QUANTIFYING THE EUROPEAN STRATEGIC AIRLIFT GAP

I. Introduction

"Transportation is a critical asset in any operation requiring the movement of military
forces"
-- (JP 4-01.4, 2000).

Background, Motivation, & Problem Statement

The identity, mission, and requirements of the North Atlantic Treaty Organization

(NATO), have been evolving since the end of the Cold War. The pace of this evolution in

mission sets has been increasing, and on a vector towards a more global and rapid

expeditionary force responding to both conflict and humanitarian need. NATO's 2006

Riga Summit established specific influence to the deployment of forces and firepower

globally as a desired mission objective for the alliance. During the summit, key limitations

to obtaining this mission capability were identified, with strategic airlift named one of

particular significance (Vasilescu, 2011:70). In 2010, the Libson Summit helped further

define NATO's developing strategic expeditionary strategy by prioritizing capability

requirements, to include airlift, and establishing the Rapid Reaction Battle Group concept

(Vasilescu, 2011:72-73).

Strategic airlift is a core capability required by NATO nations if they are to carry

out these endeavors across the globe. While the United States (U.S.), possess a tremendous

strategic airlift capability, all other NATO nations suffer a severe gap between strategic

airlift requirements and capacity. "Due to a lack of European strategic airlift capability, the

United States supported 29 European nations with over 900 airlift missions transporting

more than 20,000 short tons of cargo in 2007 alone" (Hood, 2009: 1). For reasons of sovereignty and shifting strategic focus for European partners, it is important for this reliance on the U.S. to end or be mitigated. To address airlift shortfalls, European NATO allies have collectively pooled resources through multiple initiatives. Pooled leasing of contract airlift though the Strategic Airlift Interim Solution (SALIS), the multinational purchase and operation of Lockheed C-17s via the Strategic Airlift Consortium (SAC), and the eight-nation group purchase of Airbus A400Ms constitute significant efforts in collectively addressing airlift deficiencies.

This research will attempt to quantify the strategic airlift requirement for deploying NATO Response Forces (NRF) as chartered by the alliance and compare these requirements to both current and projected airlift capacity, excluding U.S. assets. Multiple solutions to bridging the gap between requirements and capability will then be explored. As ever-increasing needs for coalition activities to support and legitimize military operations grow, clearly identifying the capability gaps of our allies and researching possible solutions will certainly net stronger partnerships and more efficient use of our own assets.

Research Focus

The research will be limited to European strategic airlift. U.S. airlift and European intratheater and/or tactical airlift capabilities will be outside the scope of this study. Any discussion or modeling and simulation was accomplished based on current or projected airlift assets and agreements. Proposed solutions focus on these same assets through expansion of capability/fleets, rather than exploring substitute aircraft and other hardware or political agreements. Although many NATO, European Union (EU) and Partners for Peace (PfP) requirements overlap, this research will focus on those of NATO, and limit requirements specific to other European entities. NRF and their deployment as outlined in NATO charters and goals will be the focus of all scenarios. A limited study of European Union Battle Groups will however aide in the framing of European objectives and serve as a comparative force structure. Pare and tailoring of deploying force requirements will be minimized, to establish capabilities needs to meet stated ambitions. Any theoretical scenarios explored through discussion or modeling will attempt to minimize U.S. and specifically Air Mobility Command (AMC) augmentation to the max extent.

Targeted Analysis

Throughout the course of researching NATO's strategic airlift requirements and projected capacity, many questions will need to be addressed. What is the requirement? What is the current capacity? What is the delta? These first 3 questions define the strategic airlift capability gap. The following questions determine how effective future airlift plans fill the defined capability gap. What is the future capacity? What is the capacity of alternatives? Answering these questions provides insight into current and future capabilities and solutions.

In framing the research questions, the following hypothesis will be explored:

- H1: The strategic airlift capability provided by Europe's current airlift fleet and resource pooling agreements of NATO and EU countries fall short of meeting stated contingency goals.

- H2: Fulfillment of the scheduled A400M procurement will adequately address NATO strategic airlift shortfalls.

- H3: Expansion of European owned C-17s will adequately address NATO strategic airlift shortfalls.

Methodology

Research for the project includes both quantitative and qualitative data. The methodology of procuring this data includes a significant literature review, algebraic mathematical analysis, interviews and deterministic modeling.

Extensive literature exists regarding the formation of NATO's developing strategies and shifting global involvement. Likewise, multiple studies estimating the airlift requirements needed to carry out these endeavors and the capabilities possessed have been completed. These studies which include those of NATO, the Joint Air Power Competence Center (JAPCC), RAND, the Naval Post Graduate School, the U.S. Air Force Air University, and those found in U.S. defense and European Union journals will serve as a base to compare derived data. It is important to note that much of this literature was written early in the strategy forming process and preceded many of NATO's airlift augmentation initiatives. This research attempts to build upon the scenarios of past studies, providing a current and projected outlook.

Algebraic estimations of the two significant variables, requirements and capacity, provide rudimentary values for this research. This information may include force structure, size, footprint and weight, along with aircraft dimensions, performance and availability. This has been the basis for past research on the topic, and has been updated for this research, then further validated through model findings.

AMC's Mobility Planner's Calculator (AMPCALC) will be used to model the deployment of NATO forces through mock scenarios based on projected requirements.

Additionally, requirements and capabilities will be determined using transportation throughput and cycle equations from Air Force Pamphlet 10-1403 and "The Algebra of Airlift" by Dr. D. Merrill and Dr. R.T. Brigantic. It is important to specify that AMPCALC is a deterministic model not a simulator. Once input parameters are established, output measures are fixed.

Qualitative data regarding NATO's airlift was gathered through interviews with prominent subject matter experts. Expertise within NATO, U.S. Air Forces Europe (USAFE), AMC A9 and RAND provided tremendous insight into the issues discussed, including assumption and limitation feasibility.

Assumptions/Limitations

Many assumptions were required to limit the scope of researching such a large and complex topic. Expanded upon in Section III, some assumptions and limitations within this study include:

- Pooling agreements remain in effect
- Deployable forces unchanged
- U.S. enroute support available for scenarios
- Air to Air refueling not used
- Stable/accurate utilization rates
- CRAF-like support not available (other than chartered AN-124s via SALIS)
- Assumed levels of multimodal support (not modeled)
- Requirements are conflict based
- SALIS remains temporary (will not be included in future fleet)
- AOR and enroute structure threat-free

Implications

Researching NATO's strategic airlift in the manner presented affords a quantified determination of the existing capability gap. The modeling served to not only identify shortfalls in capacity, but simulate the effectiveness of possible solutions. The data together with the qualitative understanding gained through expert inputs provides a clear vision of what NATO's airlift requirements are and if they can be met. The impact of deriving such information could prove beneficial to not only our European partners but to the U.S. Air Force in empowering our allies towards becoming more self-sufficient. Building Partnership (BP) endeavors among our highly developed allies is in fact as important if not more so than the traditional BP we think of involving less capable nations. Identifying limitations and solutions in their clearly developed mission sets can only help to foster better understanding and cooperation of each other and our capabilities.

II. Literature Review

Introduction

In preparation for quantifying Europe's strategic airlift gap, the researcher investigated several subject areas. In an attempt to accurately establish European requirements, a thorough investigation into NATO and EU goals and priorities was required. The evolution of desired mission capabilities and force structure pertaining to deployable contingency response was targeted for study. The transformation of NATO's anticipated global involvement is a driving force behind strategic airlift needs.

NATO Response Forces (NRFs), their stated mission, composition and ambitious timelines will be the most essential driver of future large scale European deployments. Due to the significance of the NRF, considerable review of their intended use was required. In addition to the NRF, EU Battle Groups were studied as a comparative alternative to NRF deployment. With the mission appropriately explained, the paramount importance of airlift required description. The expeditionary nature of the NRF, Battle Groups and future European endeavors is clearly benefited by intertheater strategic airlift.

Just as the airlift requirement was researched, the capability and capacity possessed was also determined. Background information on military airlift operations, assets owned or projected, and how they are managed helped define the starting point for this research. Past studies using current capabilities were closely examined to determine acceptable assumptions and findings. The projected airlift fleets of European nations were then reviewed for use in the modeling of various weapon system procurement effectiveness. In total the literature review establishes what airlift requirement exists and what capability is present or projected. Since deterministic modeling is the methodology employed for a majority of this research project, some basic background on the particular method was also explored. Each section below amplifies the literature review completed.

Strategic Transformation

The monolithic, massive and potentially immediate threat which was the principal concern of the Alliance in its first forty years has disappeared.

-From NATO's 1991 Strategic Concept

Today, the North Atlantic Treaty Organization sparsely resembles the alliance of 1949. Evolution of the organization shows significant changes in nearly all aspects of its being. Membership, mission goals, geographic focus, and strategic philosophy have all undergone noteworthy changes as the once Cold War centered alliance has attempted to adapt to a world of deepening global interdependence.

Originally formed in 1949, NATO is traditionally a military alliance joining like-minded "western" nations. With its roots serving as a response to the risk of Soviet aggression into Eastern Europe and beyond, a definitive foe and mission objective were clearly defined. Article 5 of the North Atlantic Treaty is the core of the alliance declaring that an attack on any one of its members is considered an attack on all. This article has served as the center of strategic guidance for NATO.

Despite the continuity of Article 5's importance, the strategic concepts and guidelines for NATO have experienced multiple transformations. Historians often refer to NATO's continuous evolution in terms of particular milestones or markers. Three distinct eras have been used to describe NATO's strategic evolution: the Cold War, the immediate post-Cold

8

War, and the post-9/11 periods (Halisky, 2011: 3). This approach to defining periods of NATO engagement philosophy does capture the most substantial eras of change. The beginning, end and transition away from the Cold War have undoubtedly shaped NATO most significantly. European forces structured to defend their territory from direct attack have found it difficult to transition towards the expeditionary operations that have come to define the post-Cold War international security environment. Rather than simplifying NATO's attempts to transition with three time periods, it may be more helpful to take a closer look at significant treaties and strategic concepts that have brought the alliance towards formally defining a new direction. This approach will also aide in identifying significant strategic decisions impacting the use and structure of European airlift; the purpose of this research.

Since its inception, NATO has produced several Strategic Concepts outlining the alliance's principal guidance of military means to achieve its goals and objectives. Each Strategic Concept is drafted and approved at the highest levels of NATO and national leadership. Of these official documents, the few described within this research document help outline the transformation of NATO towards an organization of increased global force projection, and organization requiring airlift to meets its objectives, and an organization fully aware of that specific requirement.

1991 Strategic Concept

The early 1990's signify perhaps the most fundamental shift in NATO strategy. A new strategy emerged from the dissolving Soviet Union, unification of Germany and the disbanded Warsaw Pact along with its ideological hostility towards NATO nations in the West. This strategy was drafted and accepted by leadership within the 1991 Strategic

Concept. The 1991 Concept describes a new security environment ripe with uncertainty regarding future risks. Acknowledging the diluted risk of territorial invasion, the 1991 Concept initiates NATO's defense strategy looking outward and globally. This begins a transformation still at work today.

Part II of the 1991 Concept describes NATO forces that must look "beyond Articles 5 & 6," guarding against risks of a "wider nature...of a global context" (1991 Strategic Concept, 1991: Part II). The outward approach to defense is further described as NATO forces are called to defend, "as far forward as possible to maintain or restore territorial integrity of Allied nations," as well as to "contribute to global security and peace by providing forces for United Nations missions" (1991 Strategic Concept, 1991: Part II). It is important to note that this Strategic Concept represents an enormous transition for NATO, yet still hinges all efforts and strategy on the primary mission of territorial defense. Throughout the document, the primary purpose of allied defense is highlighted while only small mention is made towards the support of other groups abroad. This small mention should not be understated however, as it quickly becomes a growing theme in future strategic documents.

1999 Strategic Concept

Approved by heads of state and government in Washington D.C., NATO produced its next strategic document moving the alliance towards global involvement. "The 1999 Strategic Concept further developed the ways in which NATO's military forces could be deployed, the resources available for their use, and extensively detailed the missions and guidelines for their employment" (Halisky, 2011: 5). Most significant is the 1999 Concept's specific mention of non-Article 5 operations. NATO further shifts from its roots

10

of European territorial defense by defining a broad approach to security and strategy, outlining not only defense but crisis response and humanitarian relief operations.

In conjunction with the types of operations within NATO's expanded mission set, the force structure, breadth of reach and timelines required begins to take shape. "The size, readiness, availability and deployment of the Alliance's military forces will reflect its commitment to collective defense and to conduct crisis response operations, sometimes at short notice, distant from their home stations, including beyond the Allies' territory" (1999 Strategic Concept, 1999: Part III). For the first time, NATO doctrine identifies deployability, mobility and strategic lift as "essential tasks." Similarly, an emphasis is placed on increasingly multinational forces working jointly to accomplish missions. In 1999 one can see the emergence of collaborative expeditionary European forces backed by rapid and flexible logistics.

Prague Capabilities Commitment

Along with the Strategic Concept, leadership in 1999 also introduced NATO's Defense Capability Initiative (DCI). Among the points of emphasis was deployability, mobility and getting forces to the crisis quickly (Prague Capabilities Commitments, 2002). Commitment to these capabilities was further strengthened at NATO's 2002 Summit in Brussels, emphasizing rapid deployment and sustainability of combat forces. This rapidly deployable focus reached a point of action with the 2002 Prague Summit Declaration. The initial statement of the declaration speaks to the self-awareness accompanying strategic change towards the greater outreach of NATO forces:

We underscore that our efforts to transform and adapt NATO should not be

perceived as a threat by any country or organization, but rather as a demonstration

11

of our determination to protect our populations, territory and forces from any armed attack, including terrorist attack, directed from abroad. We are determined to deter, disrupt, defend and protect against any attacks on us, in accordance with the Washington Treaty and the Charter of the United Nations. In order to carry out the full range of its missions, NATO must be able to field forces that can move quickly to wherever they are needed, upon decision by the North Atlantic Council, to sustain operations over distance and time, including in an environment where they might be faced with nuclear, biological and chemical threats, and to achieve their objectives. Effective military forces, an essential part of our overall political strategy, are vital to safeguard the freedom and security of our populations and to contribute to peace and security in the Euro-Atlantic region (Prague Summit Declaration, 2002).

Fielding forces that can move quickly, reacting to threats abroad and sustaining operations over distance and time all point toward the expeditionary vector of NATO strategy. This is a strategy increasingly reliant on deploying forces at distance, with great speed, characteristics increasingly indicating an airlift requirement.

The Declaration goes on to describe more specific requirements, such as the creation of NATO Response Forces (NRFs)[1]. Vaguely defined within the actual Declaration, the NRF consists of flexible, deployable, interoperable and sustainable land, sea and air elements ready to move quickly to wherever needed (Prague Summit Declaration, 2002). More specific military capabilities were clearly defined within the Prague Capabilities Commitment (PCC) as a supporting document to the Prague Summit Declaration. Driving the need to define specific capabilities was the significance of NATO

---

[1]The NRF will be the focus of the quantitative research within this study and is described in greater detail within its own section of this text.

12

missions in "faraway areas" requiring forces that can be "quickly deployed to distant areas to perform a wide range or missions and to remain in theater for significant periods" (Prague Capabilities Commitment, 2002). Within the PCC, allies made specific political and military commitments to improve capabilities. Of the emphasized capabilities, strategic airlift was stressed as one of eight fields essential to military operations (Prague Capabilities Commitment, 2002). This improvement was to be acted upon both individually and collectively. Allies made commitments to acquire the capabilities defined to enable future mission accomplishment (Baykal, 2005: 47). The PCC praises the collective efforts towards achieving these goals in highlighting the European Capability Action Programme, a project group on strategic airlift, led initially by Germany (Prague Capabilities Commitment, 2002).

The PCC marked a significant step in NATO's specific commitments to collectively defining operations at strategic distance from Europe and acquiring the necessary capabilities to do so. PCC requirements continue to shape NATO strategy and procurement practices as the allies focus on clearly defined desired capabilities.

Comprehensive Political Guidance

Similar to the Prague Summit of 2002, NATO's Riga Summit in 2006, issued a Declaration outlining future challenges and goals. The Declaration indicated that the establishment of the NRF was a key development in the alliance's response to rapidly emerging crisis around the world. Likewise, the NRF is described as a catalyst for transformation and interoperability to enhance the overall quality European forces used for

13

not only NATO but also the European Union[2] (2006 Riga Summit Declaration, 2006). Using the NRF as an example of positive change, NATO's transformation is further defined through multiple initiatives. Pertaining to the increasing expeditionary mission of NATO and the capabilities required are the following:

- *improving our ability to conduct and support multinational joint expeditionary operations far from home territory with little or no host nation support and to sustain them for extended periods. This requires forces that are fully deployable, sustainable and interoperable and the means to deploy them;*

- *commitments to increase strategic airlift, crucial to the rapid deployment of forces, to address identified persistent shortages. Multinational initiatives by NATO members and Partners include the already operational Strategic Airlift Interim Solution; the intent of a consortium to pool C-17 airlift assets, and offers to coordinate support structures for A-400M strategic airlift. Nationally, Allies have or plan to acquire a large number of C-17 and A-400M aircraft. There have also been significant developments in the collective provision of sealift since the Prague Summit;* (2006 Riga Summit Declaration, 2006).

One can clearly see the more specific mention of capabilities and requirements identified as NATO pivots towards becoming a global force projector.

Again, as with the Prague Summit in 2002, the Riga Summit followed its Declaration with a more specific requirements document, the Comprehensive Political Guidance. Leaders at the Summit approved this guidance, establishing the political direction for NATO's continuing transformation for the next ten to fifteen years. This

---

[2] European force sharing and collaboration between NATO and the EU builds upon this Declaration and future NATO statements. The coexistence of European forces within both organizations and their overlapping and complimentary missions is discussed within its own section further in this study.

guidance included priorities for all alliance capability issues, planning disciplines and intelligence (Halisky, 2011: 7). Among the critical capabilities outlined was the ability to conduct a multitude of operations beyond the European continent. The CPG further defined future requirements to include the agility and flexibility to respond to complex challenges far from member states. The document stated, alliance members must have the capability to mobilize, deploy and sustain not one, but concurrent major joint operations "beyond alliance territory, on its periphery and at strategic distance" (Comprehensive Political Guidance, 2006). The CPG specified that NATO needed military forces for expeditionary operations, and that their development and ability to deploy and be sustained would be NATO's top priority Halisky, 2011: 7). Clearly the shift from Article 5 and the territorial defense of allies began to find an equal as the core strategy for alliance initiatives.

2010 Strategic Concept

Still operating from the 1999 Strategic Concept, NATO Secretary General Anders Fogh Rasmussen announced a plan to develop a new Strategic Concept for 2010. In preparation for the comprehensive Strategic Concept, a Group of Experts (GOE) chaired by former U.S. Secretary of State, Dr. Madeleine Albright was formed to conduct a strategic analysis (Halisky, 2011: 8). Of the GOE's findings, stated up front was recognition of the changing mission sets required for NATO to fulfill its charter. Simply put, "NATO's core commitment—embodied in Article 5 of the North Atlantic Treaty—is unchanged, but the requirements for fulfilling that commitment have shifted in shape" (NATO 2020, 2010). The summary of findings specifically points to broader security missions beyond alliance borders and undertaking demanding missions at strategic distance as vital to the alliance's core duty. The GOE further defined the future of NATO operations by identifying four central interrelated military missions:

1. Deter, prevent and defend against any threat of aggression in order to ensure the political independence and territorial integrity of every NATO member in accordance with Article 5 of the North Atlantic Treaty.

2. Cooperate with partners and civilian institutions to protect the treaty area against a full range of unconventional security challenges.

3. Deploy and sustain expeditionary capabilities for military operations beyond the treaty area when required to prevent an attack on the treaty area or to protect the legal rights and other vital interests of Alliance members.

4. Help to shape a more stable and peaceful international security environment by enhancing partner interoperability, providing military and police training, coordinating military assistance, and cooperating with the governments of key countries.

Accompanying these defined missions was the GOE's finding that, "a significant distance still separates potential missions and available capabilities" (NATO 2020, 2010). In response to this finding, the following recommendation was listed:

Achieve deployability and sustainability goals. Forces offered to NATO by members or partners for any mission within or beyond NATO territory should be both deployable and sustainable. To this end, Allies should restructure more of their forces away from traditional fixed territorial defence missions. Deployability also requires strategic lift, which is in short supply, although the C-17 consortium is a step in the right direction. Creating a NATO Deployment Agency is an idea that has merit and should be explored. Such an agency could take responsibility for consolidating all aspects of Alliance preparations for rapid deployment.

Following the recommendations of the GOE, the 2010 Strategic Concept was adopted by NATO as its roadmap for the next ten years. The GOE's findings and recommendations were incorporated, with the enhanced commitments to modernize and invest in key capabilities clearly highlighted. Included in the core tasks and principals was the ability to sustain concurrent major joint operations and several smaller operations for collective defense and crisis response, including those at strategic distance. Further taxing logistical resources was the commitment to develop and maintain robust, mobile and deployable conventional forces to carry out both Article 5 and expeditionary operations to include using NATO Response Forces (NRFs) (2010 Strategic Concept, 2010: Core Tasks/Principles).

The Gap Between Nations

NATO is transforming, and with the transformation, commitments to more modern expeditionary forces have been made. As an alliance, NATO has formalized their commitments and penned a strategy for interaction within a world of deepening global interdependence. Although it must be assumed that member states will adhere to collective defense obligations of the alliance, it is likely that no single nation will want to act alone to achieve military goals. It is far more likely that members will pursue multinational operations (Gray, 2012: 43). Unfortunately, not all national levels of ambition are homogenous. In fact they vary greatly across Europe. The variance includes but is not limited to, budgetary commitment to defense and the political or social support of military intervention. As an alliance attempting to modernize their forces and adapt them to an expeditionary mission, the unsymmetrical burden sharing is magnified. Just one example is the fact that Germany's economy is one third larger than that of France or Great Britain, yet

17

Germany fields 60% fewer troops capable of rapid response than either (Heisbourg, 2012: 63). Consistent and homogenous levels of ambition across the alliance are of course not likely or even a goal for that matter. A great divide between member nations in their support for defense initiatives however is a growing problem. While not all wish to participate in all operations, all are expected to contribute their fair share towards the alliance's objectives and collective defense. The divide between the U.S. and Europe is of particular interest as the EU benefits equally from global stability with its global trade numbers rivaling that of the U.S.

The Growing U.S. Divide

Taking a step back from the aforementioned NATO transformation in progress, one can easily see the disconnect between these ambitions and the current fiscally constrained environment. Through the 2002 Prague Capability Commitments there is a standing agreement among NATO nations that each will invest a minimum of 2% of their GDP to defense spending. NATO's 2010 Strategy GOE indicated that only 6 of 26 European allies spend 2% or more (NATO 2020, 2010). Budgetary information released in April of 2012 indicate the numbers may not have been that promising and are actually trending in a negative direction with only the United Kingdom and Greece reaching 2% in 2011.

Table 1: Defense Expenditures as a percent of GDP

Country / Pays	Average / Moyenne 1990 - 1994	Average / Moyenne 1995 - 1999	Average / Moyenne 2000 - 2004	Average / Moyenne 2005 - 2009	2007	2008	2009	2010	2011 e
(0)	(1)	(2)	(3)	(4)	(5)	(6)	(7)	(8)	(9)
Based on current prices / Sur la base des prix courants									
Albania	//	//	//	//	//	//	1.5	1.6	1.5
Belgium	1.9	1.5	1.3	1.1	1.1	1.2	1.2	1.1	1.1
Bulgaria (a)	//	//	//	2.2	2.4	2.2	1.9	1.7	1.4
Croatia	//	//	//	//	//	//	1.6	1.5	1.5
Czech Republic	//	//	1.9	1.5	1.4	1.4	1.6	1.3	1.1
Denmark	1.9	1.7	1.5	1.4	1.3	1.4	1.4	1.5	1.4
Estonia	//	//	//	1.6	1.7	1.8	1.8	1.8	1.7
France (b)	3.3	2.9	2.5	2.3	2.4	2.3	2.1	2.0	1.9
Germany	2.1	1.6	1.4	1.3	1.3	1.4	1.4	1.4	1.4
Greece (c)	3.9	4.1	3.3	2.9	2.7	3.0	3.2	2.6	2.1
Hungary (c)	//	//	1.7	1.3	1.3	1.2	1.2	1.1	1.0
Italy (c)	2.0	1.9	2.0	1.6	1.3	1.4	1.4	1.4	1.4
Latvia	//	//	//	1.4	1.5	1.6	1.2	1.0	1.0
Lithuania	//	//	//	1.1	1.2	1.1	1.1	0.9	0.8
Luxembourg (c)	0.7	0.7	0.7	0.5	0.6	0.4	0.4	0.5	0.5
Netherlands	2.3	1.8	1.5	1.5	1.5	1.4	1.5	1.4	1.3
Norway (d)	2.8	2.2	1.9	1.5	1.5	1.4	1.7	1.6	1.5
Poland	//	//	1.8	1.7	1.8	1.5	1.7	1.8	1.7
Portugal (c)	2.4	2.1	1.7	1.5	1.4	1.5	1.6	1.6	1.5
Romania	//	//	//	1.6	1.5	1.5	1.4	1.3	1.3
Slovak Republic	//	//	//	1.6	1.5	1.5	1.5	1.3	1.1
Slovenia	//	//	//	1.5	1.5	1.5	1.6	1.6	1.3
Spain	1.6	1.3	1.2	1.2	1.2	1.2	1.2	1.1	0.9
Turkey (c)	2.8	3.2	3.2	2.0	1.8	2.0	2.1	1.9	1.9
United Kingdom (e)	3.7	2.7	2.3	2.5	2.4	2.6	2.7	2.7	2.6
NATO - Europe *	2.5	2.1	1.9	1.8	1.7	1.7	1.8	1.7	1.6
Canada	1.8	1.3	1.2	1.3	1.3	1.3	1.4	1.4	1.4
United States (e)	4.6	3.3	3.4	4.5	4.2	5.1	5.4	5.4	4.8
North America	4.4	3.2	3.2	4.2	3.9	4.7	5.1	5.0	4.5
NATO - Total *	3.5	2.7	2.6	3.0	2.8	3.1	3.4	3.4	3.0

(Financial and economic data relating to NATO defence, 2012)

If one studies the monetary defense expenditures in real dollars below, the decreasing level of capital investment bares two disappointing indicators: 1. Overall European defense investment in 2011 fell behind the previous 4 year averages by nearly $8 billion; 2. The disparity between U.S. defense investment and Total European investment grew over $24 billion when comparing 2011 to the previous 4 year average.

Country / Pays	1995	2000	2005	2007	2008	2009	2010	2011 e
(0)	(2)	(3)	(4)	(5)	(6)	(7)	(8)	(9)
Current prices / Prix courants								
Albania	//	//	//	//	//	17356	19321	19877
Belgium (a)	131156	139711	3400	3773	4298	4048	3960	3986
Bulgaria (b)	//	//	1051	1415	1553	1273	1230	1066
Croatia	//	//	//	//	//	5356	5057	5184
Czech Republic	//	44314	52960	51283	52755	59656	50808	43328
Denmark	17468	19339	20800	22731	24410	23252	25328	24259
Estonia (a)	//	//	2568	4246	4595	3978	3922	280
France (a)(c)	238432	240752	42545	45150	45366	39190	39237	38445
Germany (a)	58986	59758	30600	31090	32824	34171	34925	34630
Greece (a)(d)	1171377	2017593	5429	5997	6896	7311	5973	4622
Hungary (d)	//	226926	318552	326205	326792	298620	280895	277146
Italy (a)(d)	31561	47100	26959	20932	22631	21946	21637	21741
Latvia	//	//	115	228	259	160	133	146
Lithuania	//	//	846	1142	1251	998	849	872
Luxembourg (a)(d)	4194	5613	196	209	146	145	187	201
Netherlands (a)	12864	14284	7693	8388	8488	8733	8472	8156
Norway (e)	22224	25722	31471	34439	35932	38960	39279	40534
Poland	//	13418	17911	21681	19672	23323	25635	26394
Portugal (a)(d)	403478	479663	2527	2418	2536	2692	2782	2598
Romania	//	//	5757	6358	7558	6785	6630	7255
Slovak Republic (a)	//	//	25537	28131	30146	972	859	766
Slovenia (a)	//	//	99084	506	566	575	583	478
Spain (a)	1078751	1264299	10497	12219	12756	12196	11132	10059
Turkey (d)(f)	302864	6248274	13840	15392	16755	19603	21241	24251
United Kingdom (g)	21439	23532	30738	34430	37127	37357	39053	39650
NATO - Europe *	184352	164349	250064	287761	313866	282240	274750	282581
Canada	12457	12314	16001	19255	21100	21828	21935	23436
United States (g)	278856	301697	503353	586106	729544	757466	785831	731879
North America	287933	309989	516557	604032	749319	776561	807123	755564
NATO - Total *	472284	474338	766621	891793	1063185	1058802	1081872	1038145

(Financial and economic data relating to NATO defence, 2012)

NATO's Secretary General Anders Fogh Rasmussen highlighted the problem in November of 2012 while addressing the NATO Parliamentary Assembly in Prague, "since 1991, the non-US share of NATO's defense spending has fallen from 35% to 23% today... this growing transatlantic gap is unsustainable," he emphasized. "It undermines the Alliance principle of solidarity. NATO is about sharing. Allies share the risks and the responsibilities, just as they share the security benefits" (NATO Press Release, 13 Nov 2012).

The growing divide between the U.S. and Europe is just as visible when viewing military capability instead of economics. The brunt of this research will delve into not only the capability gap between the U.S. and Europe, but the capability gap between European ambitions and their own capabilities. The particular focus will pertain to the European strategic airlift gap, and how it may be addressed. A brief look at European plans to combat the economic issues of defense described earlier will set the stage for discussing how Europe will deploy forces in the future.

Smart Defense

NATO faces a conundrum of growing military ambitions at strategic distances from Europe, while facing decreasing defense spending amid great defense capability gaps within the alliance. The problem is compounded when one includes the growing independence Europe seeks from the U.S., particularly in global engagements since 2001. If Europe is to fulfill its global expeditionary goals, and do so with autonomy from U.S. aide, how will it do so? According to NATO doctrine (AJP-4.4(A)): "Nations are responsible for obtaining transportation resources to deploy, sustain and redeploy their forces." NATO Logistics Policy (Ref MC 319/2) however, states that NATO and nations have a collective responsibility for movement and transportation support. There will likely be instances where the European nations of NATO find themselves involved in strictly matters of predominately European interest. Operation Unified Protector in Libya, while a success story for the alliance, was a strong indicator of NATO's reliance on U.S. military capabilities even for operations within close proximity to Europe. If the European nations of NATO are to fulfill their own global ambitions without reliance on the U.S., significant changes to their national and collective responsibilities must be made.

The 2002 Prague Capabilities Commitments initiated a significant change. An emphasis on multinational commitments and pooling of funds for equipment charted a path for smaller members of NATO to combine resources towards singularly unaffordable capabilities (Halisky, 2011: 6). In March of 2011 a NATO study for building capabilities through multinational and innovative approaches was developed to further this philosophy of pooling and collective defense (Efraimsen, 2011). From this study, NATO leadership announced an initiative of Smart Defense. Generally accepted at the 2012 Chicago Summit, Smart Defense is "a renewed culture of cooperation that encourages allies to cooperate in developing, acquiring and maintaining military capabilities to undertake the Alliance's essential core tasks agreed in the new NATO strategic concept. That means pooling and sharing capabilities, setting priorities and coordinating efforts better" (Smart Defense, 2012). The idea of Smart Defense is of particular interest to building airlift capability, as the resources required are extremely expensive to both procure and operate. The philosophy of Smart Defense is NATO's chosen path to mitigating capability gaps of the future, and its effects can be seen particularly well when the alliance's expeditionary forces and strategic airlift challenges are studied. NATO Response Force (NRF), Strategic Airlift Interim Solution (SALIS) and the Strategic Airlift Capability (SAC) are indicators of NATO's strategic vector and speak particularly well to NATO's airlift requirements and challenges.

NATO Response Forces (NRFs)

" NATO will no longer have the large, massed units that were necessary for the Cold War, but will have agile and capable forces at Graduated Readiness levels that will better prepare the Alliance to meet any threat that it is likely to face in this 21st century."

-General James Jones, then Supreme Allied Commander Europe

The NRF's Multinational Structure

In an effort to modernize NATO forces for the diverse challenges of a strategic environment spanning far beyond European territories, NATO created NRFs. Official commitments to NRFs began with the Prague Capability Commitments in 2002 (Prague Capability Commitments, 2002). Made up of multinational land, air, sea and special forces, the NRF is meant to deploy quickly wherever needed. The NRF provides an expeditionary element to NATO forces, enabling expedient activation, deployment and engagement. Elements of the NRF have been employed for security during the 2004 Greek Summer Olympics, support for the 2004 Afghan presidential elections, disaster relief Operations in the 2005 and 2006 Pakistan earthquake and floods, and in support of hurricane Katrina efforts in the U.S. in 2005 (NRF Factsheet, 2013). Past activities only required partial employment of the NRF, and in less combative engagements. NATO must be prepared however to use the full NRF in full-combat operations as outlined by the Prague Capability Commitments and recent 2010 NATO Strategic Concept.

The NRF is a prime example of NATO's collaborative efforts to field forces that would otherwise be unattainable through isolated national procurement. Specific forces for each NRF are drawn from particular nations, however, the consolidated forces producing a complete NRF and the deployment capability required is a collaborative effort in line with NATO's Smart Defense initiative. Designed to rotate on 12 month rotations for readiness, Table 3 below[3] shows upcoming NRF rotations and their national force structure. Even on a chart showing only the NRF lead nations, the multinational makeup of each NRF is clearly seen. Table 4 depicts the broad collaboration of forces used to construct each NRF.

---

[3] Tables 3 and 4 were taken from official NATO Staff Officer Orientation Course Slides, 8 May 2012.

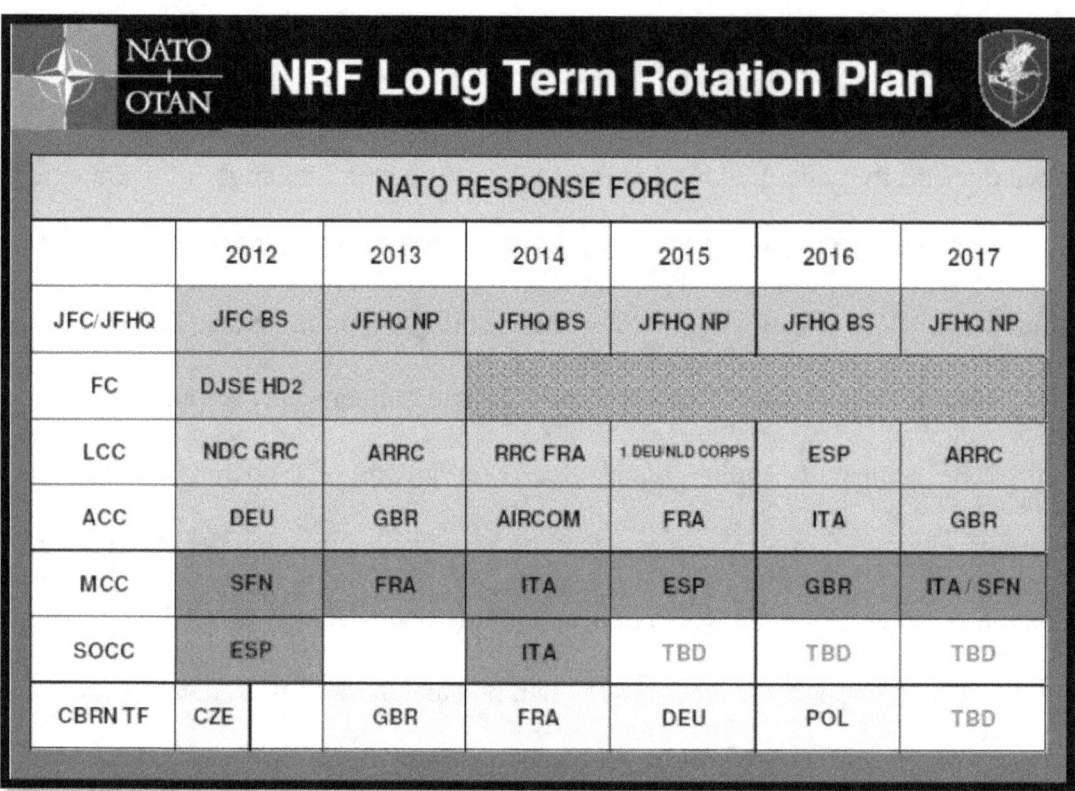

Figure 1: NRF Rotation

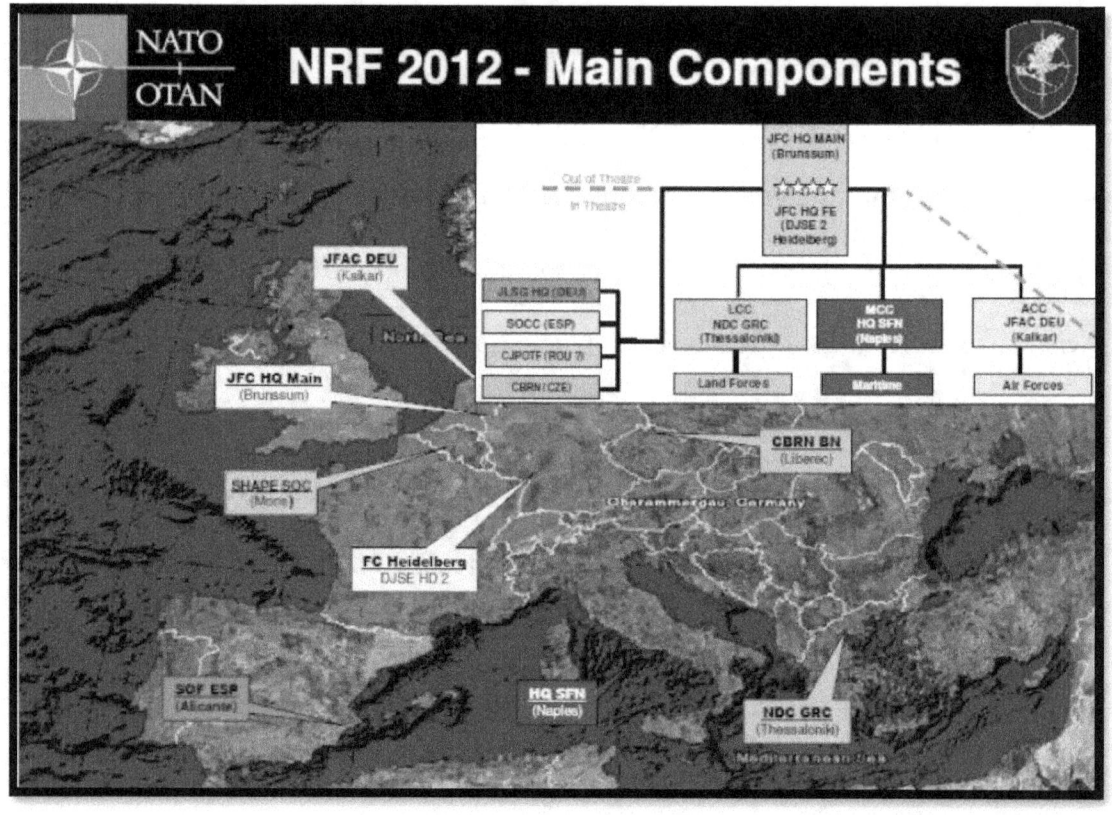

Figure 2: NRF Components by Location

As with the multinational construction of the NRF, the air and sealift required to deploy them is similarly multinational due to a lack of individual resources. Of the allies, the U.S. alone possesses the capability to deploy large NRF size forces in an expedient manner. European allies must work via Smart Defense initiatives to achieve the same level of capability if seeking to sever their reliance on U.S. air and sealift. The challenge of deploying the NRF can be seen as one studies both the size and ambitious engagement timelines.

NRF Force Structure

Within a large force upwards of 28,000 troops, NRF composition includes:

- **Immediate Response Force**: joint force of up to 13,000 high-readiness troops

    - a brigade-sized land component (around 3,000 - 5,000 soldiers) including supporting elements;

    - Maritime component based on NATO's Standing Naval Maritime Groups and Standing Naval Mine Counter Measures Groups;

    - Combat air and an air support component ;

    - Special forces;

    - Chemical, biological, radiological and nuclear defense task force

- **Response Forces**: Pool of around 15,000 follow-on forces. (NRF Factsheet, 2013)

A significant factor in NRF utilization however is the customizable size and composition, which can be uniquely modified for a given mission. For the purposes of this study, a large scale NRF deployment using a majority of total forces will be used to test airlift capacity.

Further necessitating the need for adequate logistics and airlift in particular, is

NATO's clear emphasis on rapid deployment. Force generation times are clearly defined by NATO with Notice to Move (NTM) times ranging from 72 hrs for some Immediate Response Forces, to 5 – 30 days for follow-on Response Forces (Iffert, 2012). Once in place, NRF's are capable of engaging in a full spectrum of operations independently for up to 30 days[4]. Well defined deployment movement timelines are not clearly defined. Past studies have based NRF deployment timelines on the Le Touquet joint declaration between France and the UK which states a need for military capability to deploy between 5 and 10 days (Clarke, 2004: 37). More modest and perhaps realistic timelines place troops in the Area of Responsibility (AOR), within 1 month. This 30 day figure has been the benchmark for past deployment simulations conducted by NATO and their Joint Air Power Competence Center (JAPCC) who conducts multinational expert analysis for the alliance[5]. The 30 day benchmark is further supported by the EU's similar Battle Groups, which require mobilization and deployment within 10 – 30 days (European Defence Agency, 2011), or within 60 days for major operations requiring 60,000 troops, double a full NRF (Gray, 2012)[6].

EU Battle Groups

The European Union (EU), and NATO are becoming increasingly linked in their endeavors and mutual support for each other. Although not all members of one are members of the other, the overlap between the two organizations is significant.

---

[4] NRF's may be self –sustaining for periods longer than 30 days when part of a NATO Combined Joint Task Force (NDU NRF, 2XXX).
[5] Past JAPCC simulations and others are discussed at length within the Past Studies section of this Literature Review
[6] EU Battle Groups are described later in this section

Photo Removed Due to Copyright Restictions

(European Defence Agency, 2011)

During the 1999 Helsinki European Council meeting, the EU introduced measures to create

a European Rapid Reaction Force. NATO acknowledged the EU's newfound military

ambitions, within the 2002 Prague Summit Declaration, stating, "the NRF and the related

work of the EU Headline Goal should be mutually reinforcing while respecting the

autonomy of both organizations" (Prague Summit Declaration, 2002). With both

organizations now on a path towards rapidly deployable, multinational military units, the

EU began to further define what would become EU Battle Groups. By 2006, NATO's

guidance began to site deeper interaction with EU military forces. The Comprehensive

Political Guidance endorsed by NATO heads of state and government echoed sentiments of

earlier statements and added, "NATO and the EU and their respective members states have

already agreed procedures to ensure coherent, transparent and mutually reinforcing

development of the capability requirements common to both organizations. NATO's

planning disciplines should continue to take full account of these principles, objectives and

procedures" (Comprehensive Political Guidance, 2006). Over the next three years, the EU

firmly established its Battle Group concept through the Libson Treaty and 2010 Headline

Goal. The Libson Treaty affirmed that EU member states would provide operational

27

combat resources for missions within and outside Europe for peace-keeping, humanitarian and rescue tasks, conflict prevention and post-conflict stabilization (Gray, 2012: 45). The growing similarity between EU Battle Groups and NATO NRFs was increasing. The Headline Goal 2010, set the stage for how Battle Groups would deploy. Aspirations were to launch operations within 5 days of Council approval, with mission commencement within 10 days. Target troop levels included those needed for two major stabilization and reconstruction operations supported by up to 10,000 troops for two years (Gray, 2012: 47). Other inferred troop levels more closely approximate 2000 – 2500 per Battle Group, with readiness set for two simultaneous operations (European Defence Agency, 2011). Accepting of the EU's escalating military ambitions, NATO fortified its support of the EU at the 2012 Chicago Summit. Acknowledging that the two entities share common strategic interests, and more importantly common assets, NATO accepted EU collaboration into its Strategic Concept and Smart Defense initiatives leading into 2020. The Chicago Summit Declaration clearly states NATO's most recent interests in the growing partnership:

> *NATO and the EU share common values and strategic interests. The EU is a unique and essential partner for NATO. Fully strengthening this strategic partnership, as agreed by our two organizations and enshrined in the Strategic Concept, is particularly important in the current environment of austerity; NATO and the EU should continue to work to enhance practical cooperation in operations, broaden political consultations, and cooperate more fully in capability development. NATO and the EU are working side by side in crisis management operations, in a spirit of mutual reinforcement, and in particular in Afghanistan, Kosovo and fighting piracy. NATO recognizes the importance of a stronger and more capable European defense... NATO*

will work closely with the EU, as agreed, to ensure that our Smart Defence

and the EU's Pooling and Sharing initiatives are complementary and

mutually reinforcing; we welcome the efforts of the EU (Chicago Summit

Declaration, 2012).

EU Battle Group Significance to This Study

Capabilities and intended uses of NATO NRFs and EU Battle Groups do

substantially differ. NRFs are much more oriented towards conventional combat, directed

toward larger, longer mission. Battle Groups on the other hand, lend themselves to smaller,

short duration less combat intense operations (Hamilton, 2009: 43). The readiness, delivery

and engagements of the two are not mutually exclusive however. Depending on the

contributions of member states, NRFs and Battle Groups are constituted by nearly the same

forces. This conflict of resource allocation is particularly pronounced when competing for

essential and limited resources (Molling, 2007: 3). As seen in Table 6 below, the overlap of

organizational airlift membership and capacity is substantial. This is a point of emphasis,

as each member state has its own finite airlift capabilities committed to both organizations.

This airlift has overwhelmingly been identified as a shortfall by both multinational

organizations, even as they predict future operations, independent of each other (European

Defence Agency, 2011: 3).

Photo Removed Due to Copyright Restictions

(European Defence Agency, 2011)

The Requirement for Strategic Airlift Capability

"Numerous, complex factors influence the delivery of forces and their sustainment supplies within a theater. Every theater presents different challenges, but several broad categories of factors are inherent in the theater distribution problem: theater factors, transportation factors, and movement requirement factors."

-Longhorn, Kovich, 2012

Airlift Doctrine

The European transformation from a military postured for territorial defense to one of global engagement is clearly evident. With this transformation, enhanced military capabilities have been identified as a top priority. Determining which specific capabilities are essential to European expeditionary operations is a critical step in forming how NATO will shape its future. Fortunately NATO leadership has identified critical capabilities, with strategic airlift frequently cited among the most significant. The Prague Capabilities Commitments for example, named strategic air as critical enabler of future NATO missions (Prague Capabilities Commitments, 2002).

In 2012, a study funded by the European Defense Agency (EDA), charged a multinational conglomeration of international strategists to identify the mismatch between military requirements and planned capabilities. The study included interviews of nearly 50 subject matter experts, military and civilian officials, industry managers, engineers, representatives of think tanks and prominent members of academia. Multiple seminars bringing distinguished panels of these members together was also used to produce a report though the exchange of ideas, inputs and feedback. In reference to air mobility, the report concluded the following:

> *"Air Mobility enables the deployment and sustainment of personnel and*
>
> *material at the global, regional or theatre level and across the entire*
>
> *range of operations. Air Mobility can be exerted through Air-to-Air*
>
> *Refueling (AAR), Airlift, Aero-medical Evacuation, Airborne Operations*
>
> *and Air Logistic Operations… Airlift may be necessary or preferred to*
>
> *deploy military forces worldwide in a flexible and agile manner, in a short*
>
> *period of time and with a small footprint. Particularly, inter-theatre Airlift*
>
> *provides the air bridge between the home bases and the theatre, or links*
>
> *different theatres, by using strategic air transport aircrafts, augmented by*
>
> *tactical-range air transport when needed and possible." (Gray, 2012: 50)*

The report further describes the importance of strategic airlift likely being multiplied by the increasing global interdependence and the effects of distant crises and conflicts. As NATO readies itself for a growing expeditionary mission focused on rapid response, strategic airlift's importance continues to grow. The airlift capacity required then is predominately shaped by requirements derived from the NRF and EU Battle Group concepts (European Defence Agency, 2011). Lessons learned from past NATO deployments show that force closure directly impacts operational success (AJP-4.4(A), 2005: 1101). The ambitious NRF timelines and considerable deployment distances require airlift to meet NATO's force closure goals.

Multimodal Considerations

Multimodal transportation is vital to any full spectrum logistical toolkit. Although this research focuses on strategic airlift, other modes of transportation have their place in military deployments. The use of sealift in particular becomes extremely desirable when transporting large volumes and/or s/Tons of cargo long distances. The most noticeable advantage to sealift is the cost relative to airlift. According to a center for strategic and international studies, for the cost of transporting 72,000 s/Tons of cargo 4,000 nautical miles, sealift could transport 55 times that amount (Lindstrom, 2007: 41). There is a reason a vast majority of freight is moved via sea and/or land world-wide. Even with relatively slow average speeds of 12-18 Kts, sealift of large amounts may actually improve cargo velocity. The case for multimodal use of strategic sea and airlift was proven as the U.S. moved nearly 7,000 Mine Resistant Ambush Protected Vehicles (MRAP) to Afghanistan in. Before the House Armed Service Committee in 2011, then U.S. TRANSCOM Commander, General Duncan McNabb testified that the use of multimodal delivery not only saved nearly $400 million, but increased the velocity of delivery to the warfighter (McNabb, 2011).

There is no doubt that deployment by means other than airlift will be prominent in future NATO deployments. With member state's modern port facilities, and deep-water access, Europeans will be inclined to utilize sealift for deployment operations. Some experts state that sealift will provide the large majority of transport capacity for NRF movements (Clarke, 2004: 45). This is a fact not unnoticed by NATO leadership, as strategic sealift remains a listed critical capability just as strategic airlift is (Prague Capability Commitment, 2002). There are many limitations to sealift as well however, and a current shortfall of strategic sealift for NATO allies is just one.

Sealift does provide large volumes of cargo at relatively cheap costs. Where lengthy build-up times and significant costal port access at or near the warfighter's base of operations is available, sealift makes perfect sense. Unfortunately the onload/offload times, movement speed, infrastructure requirements and port access all hamper sealifts viability for many deployment scenarios. Current analysis and war-gaming has shown that sealift platforms do not support future war-fighting concepts" (Objective Force Mobility, 2007).

In general sealift is significantly slower than airlift. This is a limiting factor during rapid response deployments, which are specified as critical to NATO through multiple Strategic Concepts. For two of the scenarios that will be modeled later in this research, sealift accounts for a portion of the deployment, however, one can see below in Figures 1 & 2, the relatively lengthy delivery times for sealift. Added to the time below would be the lengthy build-up and on load times, significant mass offload times, and for a landlocked APOD, the additional movement time/resources needed to get cargo from port to the warfighter. As stated earlier and within AJP-4.4, NATO deployments have shown that force closure has a direct impact on the ability of the commander to implement his concept of operations" (AJP-4.4(A), 2005: 1101). In fact, past NATO force deployments demanding the delivery of men and equipment rapidly, found the use of sealift assets "relatively limited" (Baykal, 2005: 22).

Figure 3: Atlantic APOD Sealift

The above results depict Scenario 1 of this research using a centrally located European port to deliver a NRF to the Bahamas. http://www.searates.com/reference/portdistance/

Figure 4: Central African Sealift

The above results depict Scenario 2 of this research using a centrally located European port to deliver a NRF to the closest deep water port to Rwanda. http://www.searates.com/reference/portdistance/

Further compounding the restrictions to sealift is accessibility. Many sealift resources require deep-water ports. This infrastructure while plentiful in Europe, is limited geographically to modern industrial nations and nearly absent to most nations in the southern hemisphere (Objective Force Mobility, 2007). It is not hard to imagine a majority of NRF scenarios that will take place in areas with less than ideal port infrastructure support. The limited number of these ports leads to many anti-access measures and jeopardizes the deployment of war-fighting forces such as the NRF (Objective Force Mobility, 2007). Within the context of port access, proximity to the area of operations is also a substantial limitation. Even with port access, this is typically costal, and can be far from the warfighter. Some areas of operation are land locked, severely hampering the relevance of sealift (Lindstrom, 2007: 41). Operations in Kosovo and Afghanistan are merely two real-world examples.

Sealift, as well as land transportation have their place in the deployment of forces. The proper mix of transportation modes for varying contingencies must be carefully examined. This research will focus on the air mode of transport, as it is just one, yet perhaps the most critical. When speaking of airlift importance, a former Chairman of NATO's Military Committee stated, "strategic lift, airlift and sealift – primarily airlift for the short notice deployments and those with a very short timeline – is very crucial" (Henault, 2007).

Strategic vs. Tactical Airlift Requirements

Airlift and particularly strategic airlift is critical to European ambitions. This is an important distinction, as the tactical intra-theater airlift is well established in Europe. The fleets required for short range, European territorial defense are adequately in place. Large fleets of European C-130s and C-160s provide significant capability in this regard[7]. Three factors energize the need for increased strategic lift capacity: heavy lift capability, outsize cargo capacity, and extended range carrying each. A shortfall exists for long-range, heavy-lift aircraft, as the most European nations possess very few (Vlachos-Dengler, 2007: 17). The growth of outsized cargo is also increasing. Figures 3 & 4 show the swelling of equipment, driving a need for larger transport vessels.

Photo Removed Due to Copyright Restictions

Figure 5: Past Equipment

(Efraimsen, 2013)

---

[7] European airlift fleets are described in greater detail within Section II and Appendix A.

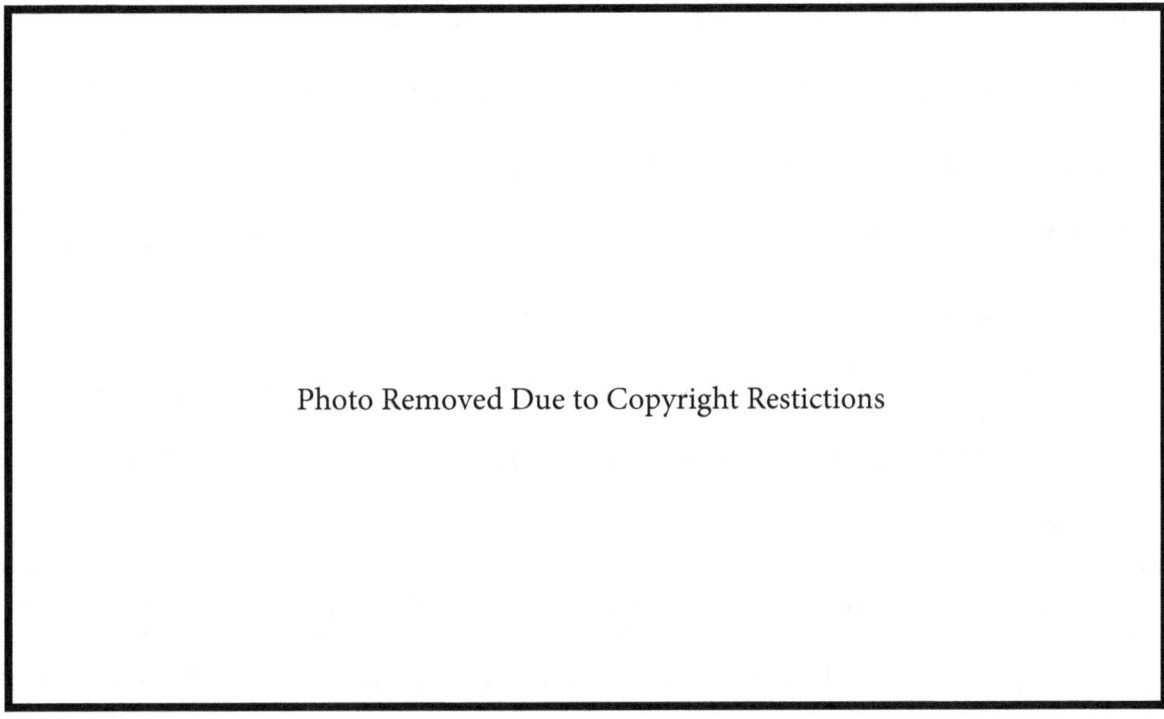

Figure 6: Current/Future Equipment

(Efraimsen, 2013)

Strategic outsize airlift capabilities are critical to future expeditionary operations.

Europeans do not currently have the capability to move their own requirements via air using

their own resources. Allies have instead relied on a mix of commercial and foreign military

assets such as chartering Antonov An-124s or relying on the U.S. Air Force (Vlachos-

Dengler, 2007: 19). This shortfall is really at the crux of this research, and will be

quantified.

The Strategic Airlift Shortfall

Deficiencies in strategic airlift for NATO are acute and acknowledge. Examples of

European requirements for strategic airlift include, but are not limited to, operations in

Darfur, the Balkans, Afghanistan, Pakistan, Libya and hurricane Katrina relief. In both

Pakistani and U.S. relief operations, NATO was required to use large numbers of tactical resources to consolidate items for strategic lift (Hood, 2009: 5).

The strategic airlift shortfall is not hidden from European leadership. The following are just a few public admissions of the capability gap.

- 1999 Kosovo: *"Strategic airlift was also one of the major European deficiencies identified in the aftermath of the Kosovo campaign."* (Vlachos-Dengler, 2007: 17)

- 2002 Prague Summit: *"Alliance members decided to reduce drastically the list of DCI shortfalls…strategic airlift remained on that shortlist"* (Vlachos-Dengler, 2007: 17)

- 2003 Helsinki: *"The Helsinki Progress Catalogue 03 highlights severe shortfalls in European strategic lift assets in response to the Headline Goal 2003."* (European Defence Agency, 2011:13).

- 2007 NATO Supreme Allied Commander Europe's (SACEUR) Minimum Military Requirements Study for NATO Response Force: *"The United States and NATO have repeatedly called on nations to increase their strategic airlift capability, but most NATO nations do not have the resources to procure and operate their own strategic airlift. Nevertheless, the strategic airlift requirements of our NATO Allies continue to grow. The need for strategic airlift is particularly acute."* (National defense authorization bill proposal, 2007: 1)

- 2011 Japan: *"This shortfall is well recognized. Most recently, the absence of strategic airlift slowed Europe's ability to respond effectively to provide disaster assistance to tsunami victims in Southeast Asia."* (Flournoy, 2005: 87)

- 2012 Afghanistan: *"Current European transport fleet have demonstrated substantial shortfalls in this regard (strategic airlift), as epitomized by the operations in Afghanistan where EU member states had to rely on external*

contractors for strategic movements." (Gray, 2012: 54).

This research will attempt to quantify the current shortfall, and provide possible solutions

through simulation and modeling.

National Responsibility

At the core of this research is the premise that European nations desire to operate

autonomously from outside nations, including the U.S. The most significant contributor to

NATO capabilities by far, the U.S. also has incentive to support a more self-sufficient

Europe. In terms of the NRF, European member states have assembled world-class forces

that have become fully operational in 2009. Europeans do not however, possess the means

to transport a full NRF a considerable distance in the expedient manner outlined in their

own goals.

In terms of airlift, NATO doctrine supports both the national responsibility of each

member state, and the collective initiatives outlined in the Smart Defense initiatives.

According to NATO doctrine (AJP-4.4(A), 2004), "Nations are responsible for obtaining

transportation resources to deploy, sustain and redeploy their forces." NATO logistics

polity states that NATO nations have a collective responsibility for movement and

transportation (Efraimsen, 2011). When the deployment of the NRF is considered, the later

statement of collective responsibility would seemingly take precedence as the NRF deploys

as a multinational force. Unfortunately even through pooling of current resources,

European members of NATO (who compose the NRF) do not have the capacity to

adequately deploy at strategic distance. Even within moderate distance, Operations Allied

Force and Unified Protector demonstrated the heavy reliance of European allies on U.S.

strategic transportation. An assessment of airlift by the Joint Air Power Capabilities Center noted that, "The majority of European NATO nations have little or no Strategic AT and are reliant upon the US military or civilian charter, furthermore, many nations misuse Tactical AT as a stopgap for their lack of Strategic AT thus impacting on the Tactical AT requirement" (NATO Air Transport Capability, 2011: 32).

Current Airlift Capability

National Responsibility

As an alliance, NATO does not own any strategic transportation assets of its own. NATO doctrine states that nations are responsible for obtaining transportation resources to deploy, sustain and redeploy their forces (AJP-4.4(A), 2004). As such, a majority of members have historically procured equipment based on their own national requirements, rather than those of the alliance (Efraimsen, 2012). This is fact is thoroughly evident when seeing that nearly 89% of all NATO strategic airlift aircraft are owned by the U.S., who have had an established global military range of goals for quite some time (NATO Air Transport Capability, 2011).

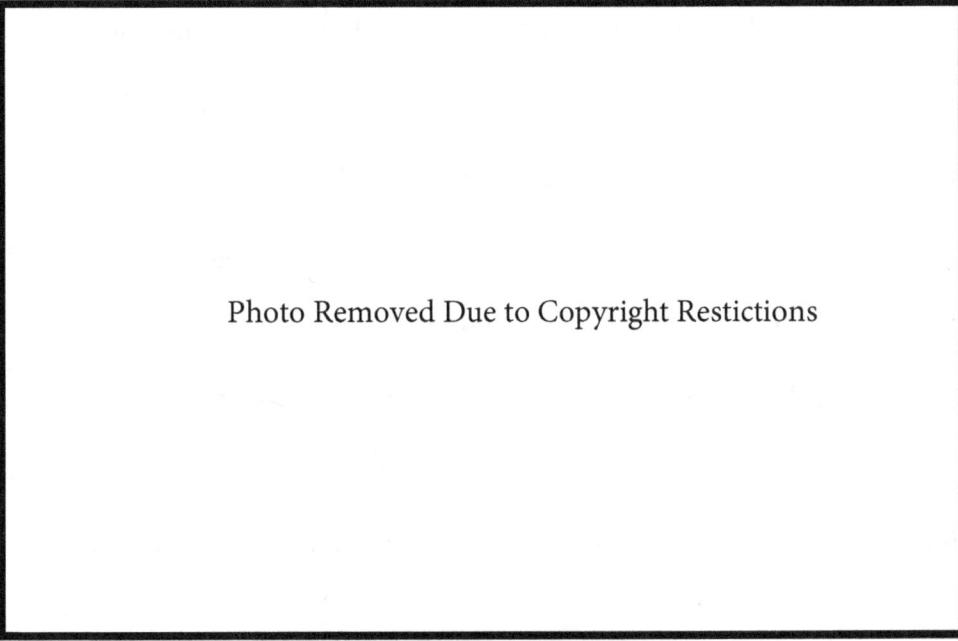

Table 6 from the JAPCC Air Transport Assessment. Note: The A400M although having strategic capabilities was listed as a tactical aircraft procurement by JAPCC. A400M orders decrease U.S. % of strategic aircraft from 89% to 70%.

As discussed, NATO's ambitions have been undergoing significant transformations, and so to have alliance transportation requirements. The current fleet of European strategic airlifters do not match alliance ambitions.

Airlift Coordination

The fact of the matter is that European airlift fleets represent alliance goals of twenty years ago. The current fleet is composed primarily of older Lockheed C-130B/E/H, Boeing CV-22/MV-22, Transall C-160 and Alenia C-27J tactical aircraft. True strategic European lift consists of only 7 UK C-17s and 3 additional C-17s from the Strategic Airlift Capability (SAC). Limited strategic lift is provided by Boeing KDC-10, Airbus A310,

A340 and A330 Multi-role Tanker Transport (MRTT) aircraft[8]. MRTT use is hampered however by stringent loading/unloading criteria and loading equipment, outsize cargo capacity limitations and rolling stock limitations. These MRTT aircraft while providing an exceptional value in their air refueling, passenger and bulk cargo capability, would likely provide a majority of deployment air-to-air refueling, and passenger movement rather than the strategic lift for NRF deployment of equipment. The passenger lift capability provided is critical, and one of the deployment capabilities not currently seen as a strategic lift shortfall. Helping to maximize the European use of available airlift are two strategies. The first is to properly coordinate the multinational fleet of aircraft that are available for alliance needs.

European Air Transport Command (EATC)

EATC is a multinational HQ created in response to the Member Nations' willingness to share resources and deepen cooperation to achieve increased synergy. The EATC will exercise operational control of air transport assets under a single command. Efficiency and increased collective capability will be achieved by synchronizing and optimizing the preparation, use and planning of joint airlift capabilities. The EATC promotes interoperability and standardization. By identifying each element of airlift operations, each member is able to select the functions it wishes to delegate and which it wishes to retain. EATC requires information systems to maintain effective control of AT assets under its operational control. It is developing the Management European Air Transport (MEAT) system to handle multinational planning, tasking, execution and management of all flights operated under its authority. EATC draws on EAG and other

---

[8] An expanded list of European airlift assets as described by the JAPCC is located in Appendix A of this report.

expertise to develop its own procedures and standards.

Movement coordination Center Europe (MCCE)

The MCCE is a multimodal transport center, created by merging the former EACC and SCC. It seeks to provide coordination of Air, Land and Sea Transport between member Nations by matching requests with declared available capacity. The MCCE has enjoyed considerable success and is highly regarded by many Nations. The organization is an excellent example of what can be achieved through collocation and practical coordination.

Air Transport, Air-to-Air Refueling and other Exchanges of Services (ATARES) is a mechanism to enable exchanges in kind of AT, Air Refueling and other services between member Nations, based on an accounting system whose currency is the "equivalent C-130 flying hour". Implemented by the MCCE, it is not an organization in itself but is an excellent example of a simple and effective way of enhancing synergy and cost effectiveness.

Airlift Augmentation

The second strategy of mitigating the European airlift shortfall is through two forms of multinational augmentation. Both the Strategic Airlift Interim Solution (SALIS), and the Strategic Airlift Capability (SAC), aim to provide large strategic airlifters to European partners that they could otherwise not afford procuring on their own. Each of the two initiatives provide Antonov AN-124 and C-17 aircraft respectively, with much larger cargo capabilities than that available within the nationally owned European fleet[9].

---

[9] The UK does have its own 7 C-17 aircraft. Despite this ownership, the UK does still participate in SALIS to further augment their strategic airlift needs.

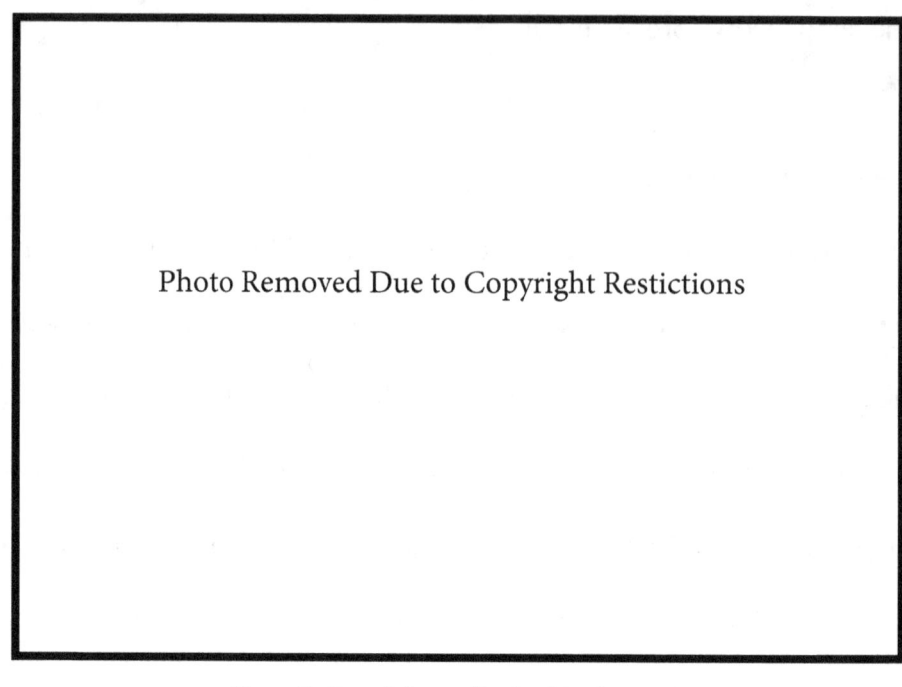

Photo Removed Due to Copyright Restictions

Figure 7: Aircraft Range/Payload Performance

(European Defence Agency, 2011)

Photo Removed Due to Copyright Restictions

Figure 8: Aircraft Cargo Hold

(European Defence Agency, 2011)

Strategic Airlift Interim Solution (SALIS)

SALIS provides varying levels of access to 6 AN-124 aircraft operated by SALIS GmbH, a Russian subsidiary of Volga Dnepr. Two aircraft are contracted on a part-time charter, two more are assured within six days' notice, and two more on nine days' notice. The contract also specifies as minimum of between 2000 and 2450 flying hours per year[10].

SALIS characteristics are outlined within a Memorandum of Understanding (MOU) between 12 NATO allies and two Partnership for Peace (PfP) nations: Belgium, the Czech Republic, France, Germany, Greece, Hungary, Luxembourg, Norway, Poland, Slovakia, Slovenia, the United Kingdom, Finland and Sweden. Coordination for the use of SALIS aircraft is conducted by the MCCE's SALIS Coordination Cell in Eindhoven, Netherlands (SALIS, 2013).

Strategic Airlift Capability (SAC)

Made of ten NATO allies and two PfP nations, SAC represents the reality of European efforts towards greater cooperation and NATO's Smart Defense initiative. SAC possess three C-17, that are owned, maintained, crewed and operated by personnel from all participating nations via the multinational Heavy Airlift Wing (HAW) based in Papa, Hungary. The crews and support personnel are trained to standards agreed upon by all members. Each participating nation owns a portion of allocated flying hours on the fleet.

These strategic assets can be used to meet national, NATO, EU, UN or other international requirements as agreed up on by a council of the members. Although not a NATO specific organization, NATO's Support Agency (NSPA), directs acquisition, and manages the SAC fleet.

---

[10] The countries have committed to using the aircraft for a minimum of 2000 flying hours per year for 2013 and for a minimum of 2450 flying hours for 2014.

45

SAC represents a fantastic example of how the pooling of not only asset access can contribute to meeting alliance requirements, but how pooling acquisition and management can work as a force multiplier. Highly publicized as an example of things to come for NATO and Europe, NATO's Airlift Management Programme manager, Mr. Gunnar Borch has the following to say about SAC:

> *The successful establishment of the SAC Program can be largely explained by the timeliness of an initiative consisting of pooling resources in order to acquire maximum airlift capability for many nations, in a restrictive budgetary environment. The sound concept on which our programme has been founded matches perfectly the new NATO strategy, investing in more flexible and mobile armed forces, while capitalizing on collaborative defence projects and avoiding capabilities duplication. Therefore, it is my deep conviction that SAC and its historic partnership of twelve NATO and PfP countries will constitute an example for future cooperation between nations (Borch, 2013).*

Taken from the European Defense Agency's February 2011 report, Figure 7 below depicts the nations involved in the cooperative initiatives described (EDA, 2011).

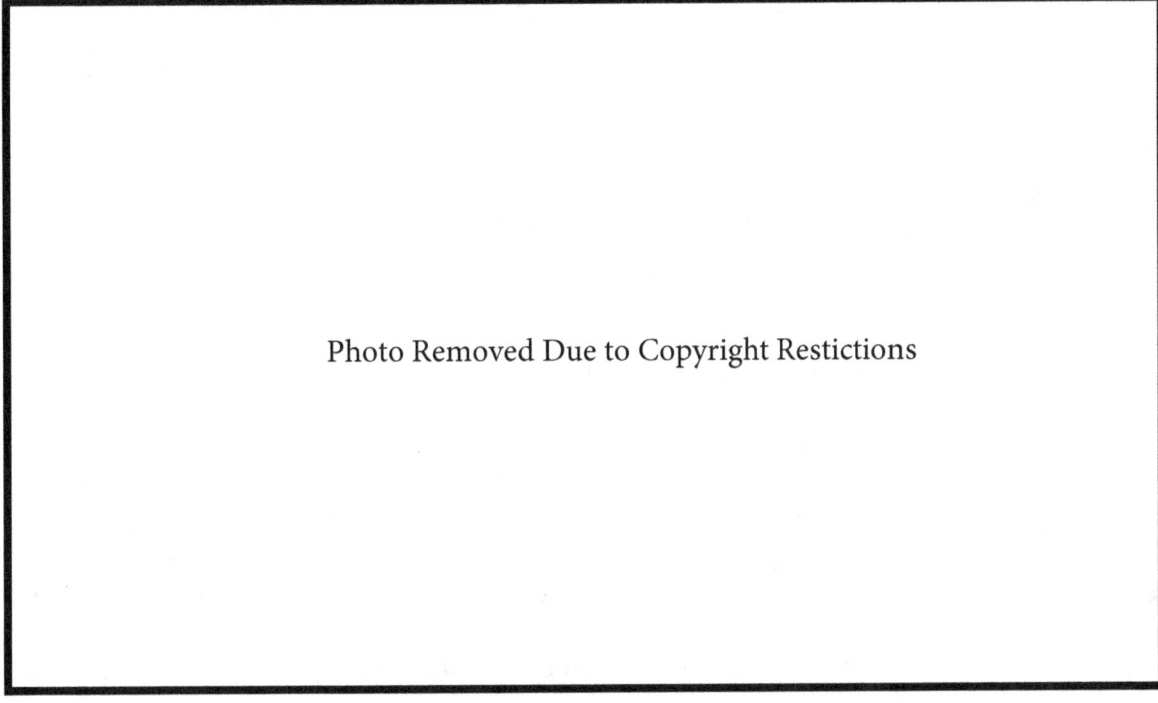

Photo Removed Due to Copyright Restictions

Figure 9: European Cooperative Initiatives

(European Defence Agency, 2011)

Past Studies

Many references have been made to NATO's strategic airlift shortfall. From official documents and declarations to statements from leadership, the capability gap is acknowledged. Quantifying the airlift gap has proven to be somewhat challenging due to the wide range of both requirements and capability variables. This research attempts to quantify NATO's strategic airlift requirement, building upon a study conducted in 2005 by the JAPCC. The most comprehensive and direct study on deploying the NRF, the JAPCC study provides many of the variables and assumptions that could only be gleaned from internal NATO access to requirements and leadership. All data presented within this research is unclassified.

Neither NATO nor EU has ever deployed a full NRF or Battle Group. The composition and philosophy behind each promotes their tailored approach to force structure as needed. Nevertheless, employing a full NRF or Battle Group is an ambitious and stated goal. The following studies give some insight as to varying methods of quantifying the lift required, and the varying results that have presented themselves. Unless otherwise noted, Maximum on Ground (MOG) and airfield throughput were not binding constraints.

Belgium's Royal Defense College, 2004

In 2004, Belgium's Royal Defense College researched deployment of European forces for peace keeping forces. The requirements were derived from the EU's Headline Goal Task Force guidelines. From these guidelines, the researchers estimated 20% of the EU Battle Group would be moved by air a distance of 4,000 kilometers over the course of 60 days. This translates to roughly 40,000 s/Tons and 60,000 troops. Notice this study used C-17 equivalents, a platform that Europe possess in limited numbers.

Table 6: 2004 Belgian Royal Defense College Study

Photo Removed Due to Copyright Restictions

(Hood, 2009)

RAND, 2003

A study conducted by RAND for the U.S. Army in 2003 researched the deployability of a medium Brigade with a 96 hour force closure. While the 4 day deployment window does not translate directly to a NATO NRF deployment benchmark, this study may be indicative of the requirement necessary to move the Immediate Response

Force portion of the NRF. Note the report for this study indicates the use of 80 C-17

aircraft, but does not express the utilization rate of each.

Table 7: 2003 Rand Study

Photo Removed Due to Copyright Restictions

(Davis & Shapiro, 2003).

To relate this more closely to NATO NRF deployment standards, simple extrapolation

shows a better relative comparison. Though these means, one could deduce that given a

deployment period of 30 days, this 15,000 s/Ton requirement could be moved with 11 C-

17s. This of course does not take into account each aircraft cubing out in terms of volume.

This is a substantial assumption given this study analyzed the movement of 300 combat

vehicles of 20 s/Tons each, and 900 soft-skinned support vehicles (Davis & Shapiro, 2003).

U.S. Army Transformation Plan

U.S. Army Transformation plans call for their brigades to be deployed anywhere in

the world in 4 days, a division in 5 days and 5 divisions within 30 days (Objective Force

Mobility, 2007). The study described, researched deploying U.S. Army light infantry

brigades, a heavy armor brigade and a stryker brigades strategic distances. Although the

timelines are for this study do not match European benchmarks, it does represent a force

deployment similar in size to a European Battle Group or smaller NRF land component.

49

Photo Removed Due to Copyright Restictions

Indicate data not obtained directly from the study, but derived from the data given to provide a more similar data-set to analyze.

(Objective Force, 2007)

Joint Air Power Competence Center (JAPCC), 2005

In 2005, the JAPCC conducted an airlift simulation using NATO's Allied Deployment and Movement System (ADAMS). The study modeled NATO's (2005) airlift capability against two theoretical NRF deployments. The first scenario included an island destination roughly 4100 NM from central Europe[11]. The second scenario consisted of a large NRF deployment to a landlocked location in central Africa, approximately 3,300 NM from central Europe (Massai, 2005).

NRF requirements for the simulation were difficult to predict given the adaptable nature of NRF requirements and the rotating multinational forces comprising each NRF. The JAPCC researchers decided to structure requirements between a full NRF deployment based on CJSOR requirements and recently conducted NATO deployment exercises. Through ADAMS, approximated forces were accurately constructed using NATO's LOGBASE for deployment-related data and their Force Data Management module. The requirements totaled approximately 100,000 s/Tons and 22,000 personnel per scenario[12]. Although the specific forces generated are classified, the study did conclude that nearly

---

[11] For the purposes of the simulation, Ramstein AB, Germany was used as the major APOD for both scenarios.

[12] Exact requirements are described and analyzed in Section III of this study.

60% of the required cargo required outsize capable aircraft (Massai, 2005).

NRF sea and air-components were assumed to be self-deployed, with the focus of this study being the air transportation of the simulated NRF land-component. The importance of sealift was strongly emphasized by the study, yet the researchers identified the feasibility of deploying the NRF with airlift as their goal. The timeline for deployment was 1 month, based on stated NATO goals, and past exercise benchmarks. Airlift assets included those likely to be used in a fully-backed NATO campaign, including U.S. and chartered assets. Air fleets included: A-310, TU-154, KDC-10, KC-135, C-5, C-17, VC-10, C-130 and AN-124s (Massai, 2005).

Results showed that despite significant strategic airlift support from the U.S. and charter aircraft, deploying the NRF within 1 month was not possible. The results were generally accepted by logistics analysts, with the most significant criticism surrounding the likelihood of such a deployment relying so heavily on airlift vs. a more multi-modal approach (Efraimsen Interview, 2013). Below in Table 10 are some of the basic requirements from the study.

Table 9: JAPCC 2005 Study

JAPCC 2005 Requirements			
(Island APOD)			
Cargo (sTons)	Personnel	Distance (NM)	Closure (Days)
77,000	25,000	4,100	30
(Landlocked APOD)			
Cargo (sTons)	Personnel	Distance (NM)	Closure (Days)
93,000	20,000	3,300	30

Projected Airlift Capability

As described throughout this literature review, European allies currently suffer from a strategic airlift shortfall. Although significant capacity does exist in their modern air forces, the current airlift fleet capacity simply does not meet stated deployment goals. Through cooperative measures and fleet augmentation, the Europeans have attempted to mitigate their shortfall's effect. To truly fill the airlift gap however, new fleet procurement with an emphasis on strategic lift is necessary.

MRTT Expansion

European militaries have two significant aircraft orders complete that may substantially if not completely fulfill their requirements in terms of allowing European allies to meet stated alliance goals on their own. The first movement towards a more robust strategic fleet is the expansion of MRTT platforms. As of January 31st, 2013, the UK as already received 3 of its ordered 14 MRTT A-330 aircraft (Airbus Military, 2013). The A-330 is a substantial strategic lift vehicle in terms of bulk cargo and passenger delivery. Similar to the A-330, Germany has ordered 2 A-340 MRTT aircraft. These MRTT A-330s and A-340s build upon the A-310s already in the European fleet, predominately with Germany.

The additional MRTTs do help with the airlift gap, but have pronounced short-comings as strategic lifters. First, the rich are getting richer so-to-speak. Germany and certainly the UK already own a majority of the strategic airlift assets in Europe. While the addition of the MRTTs do boost allied capacity, it is a fact that 80% of airlift capability already sits with 8 nations (European Defence Agency, 2011: 28).

Photo Removed Due to Copyright Restictions

Figure 10: Cargo Capacity by Nation

(European Defence Agency, 2011)

Just as the European's want to avoid relying on U.S. or Canadian aide for engagements of

their own interests, they also want to avoid an oligopoly of airlift within the European

Union.

Secondly, MRTT use is hampered by stringent loading/unloading criteria and loading equipment, outsize cargo capacity limitations and rolling stock limitations. These MRTT aircraft while providing an exceptional value in their air refueling, passenger and bulk cargo capability, would likely only provide a majority of deployment air-to-air refueling, and passenger movement rather than the strategic lift for NRF deployment of equipment. As mentioned earlier, past simulations show more than 60% of cargo requiring outsized lift and/or rolling on/offload (Massai, 2005). Along these same lines, these MRTT aircraft require large airfields with lengthy, clean runways for operation at significant gross-weights.

European Civil Reserve Air Fleet (CRAF)

Despite its large organic airlift fleet, the U.S. is still heavily augmented by its own agreements with civilian carriers for strategic airlift. The Civil Reserve Air Fleet (CRAF) may account for nearly of 60% of airlift for large-scale global engagements according to (Grismer, 201: 165). Like the Americans, European allies have the benefit of strong national airlines throughout the continent. There is an enormous pool of capacity for possible use. Unlike the U.S. however, European militaries do not possess the organic strategic fleet to serve as the primary load bearing capability for deployment.

Another issue with deployability relying on civilian carriers is access. Civilian carriers may not always be readily available for the services needed on short notice. In times of crisis demand for airlift globally may dramatically increase. This was the case during the 2004 tsunami disaster for example. The global demand for humanitarian aid delivery was immense (Vlachos-Dengler, 2007: 20). Additionally, civilian operations in contingencies of high-intensity conflict may present severe limitations. Civilian companies

54

may significantly restrict operating requirements or choose not to participate at all (Vlachos-Dengler, 2007: 21).

Strategic Airlift Capability (SAC) Expansion

SAC and its Heavy Airlift Wing (HAW) currently operate three C-17s. Membership currently consists of 10 NATO nations: Bulgaria, Estonia, Hungary, Lithuania, the Netherlands, Norway, Poland, Romania, Slovenia and the United States, and two Partnership for Peace (PfP) nations: Finland and Sweden. Together with the UK's seven C-17 aircraft Europe has substantial direct access to a small but capable fleet of true strategic airlifters.

There has been interest among current member to expand membership. Membership in the airlift fleet remains open to other countries upon agreement by the consortium members (NATO.int: SAC, 2013). Rather than simply including more members to share time on the existing C-17s however, this research will examine the strategic effect of expanding the number of C-17s in the HAW. Developing a large C-17 fleet is highly unlikely for any single European nation in this time of fiscal difficulty, however pooling may be an option. Given the success of SAC and the interoperability already inherent in C-17 operation, expansion of SAC's fleet must be considered as a potential option to fulfilling European airlift needs.

A400M Procurement

The use expansion of MRTT aircraft and civilian chartered augmentation are helpful but not ideal options for truly fulfilling European requirements. The SALIS charter is the most significant stop-gap for the airlift shortfall. As aptly named however, SALIS is intended to be an expensive "interim solution" until proper procurement of new aircraft can be completed. The answer appears to be delivery of the EADS A400M. The A400M offers cargo carrying capability greater than a C-130J, yet less than a C-17.

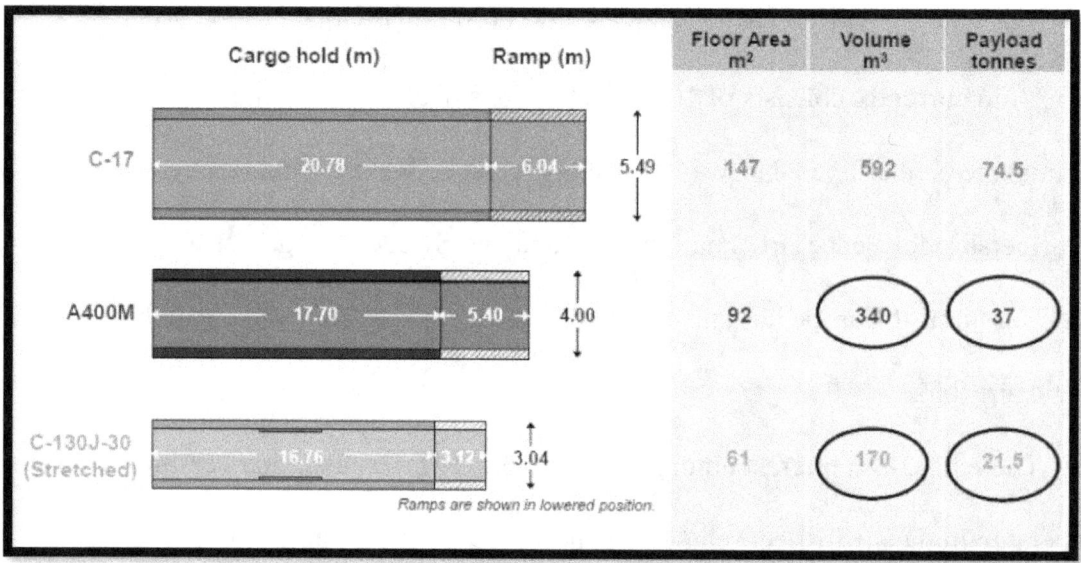

Figure 11: Aircraft Cargo Hold

(A400M, 2012)

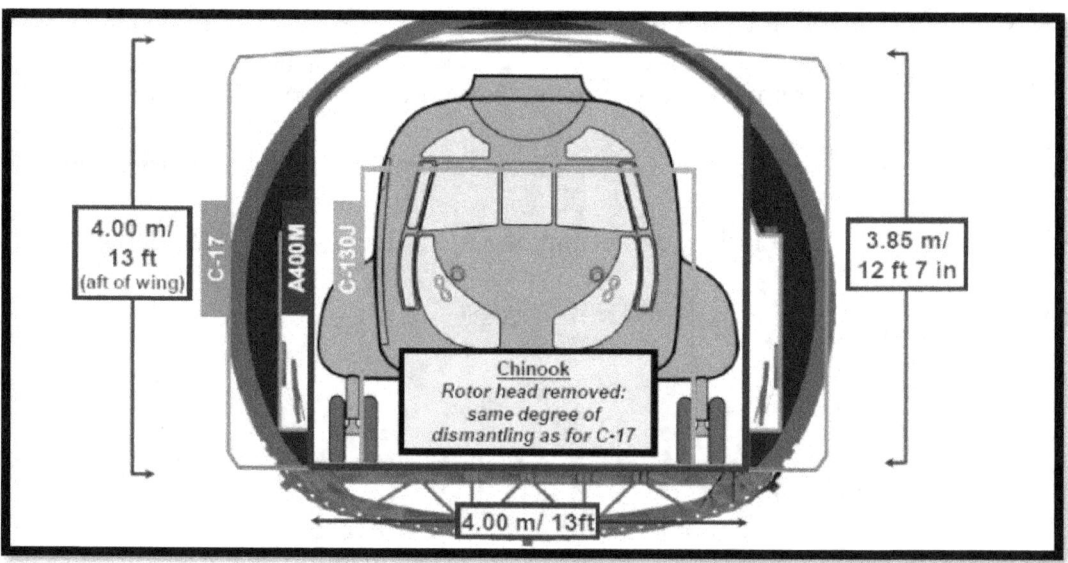

Figure 12: Aircraft Cargo Hold Cross-section

(A400M, 2012)

Likewise, the A400M can operate at strategic range at high velocity, which may result in expedited force closure times.

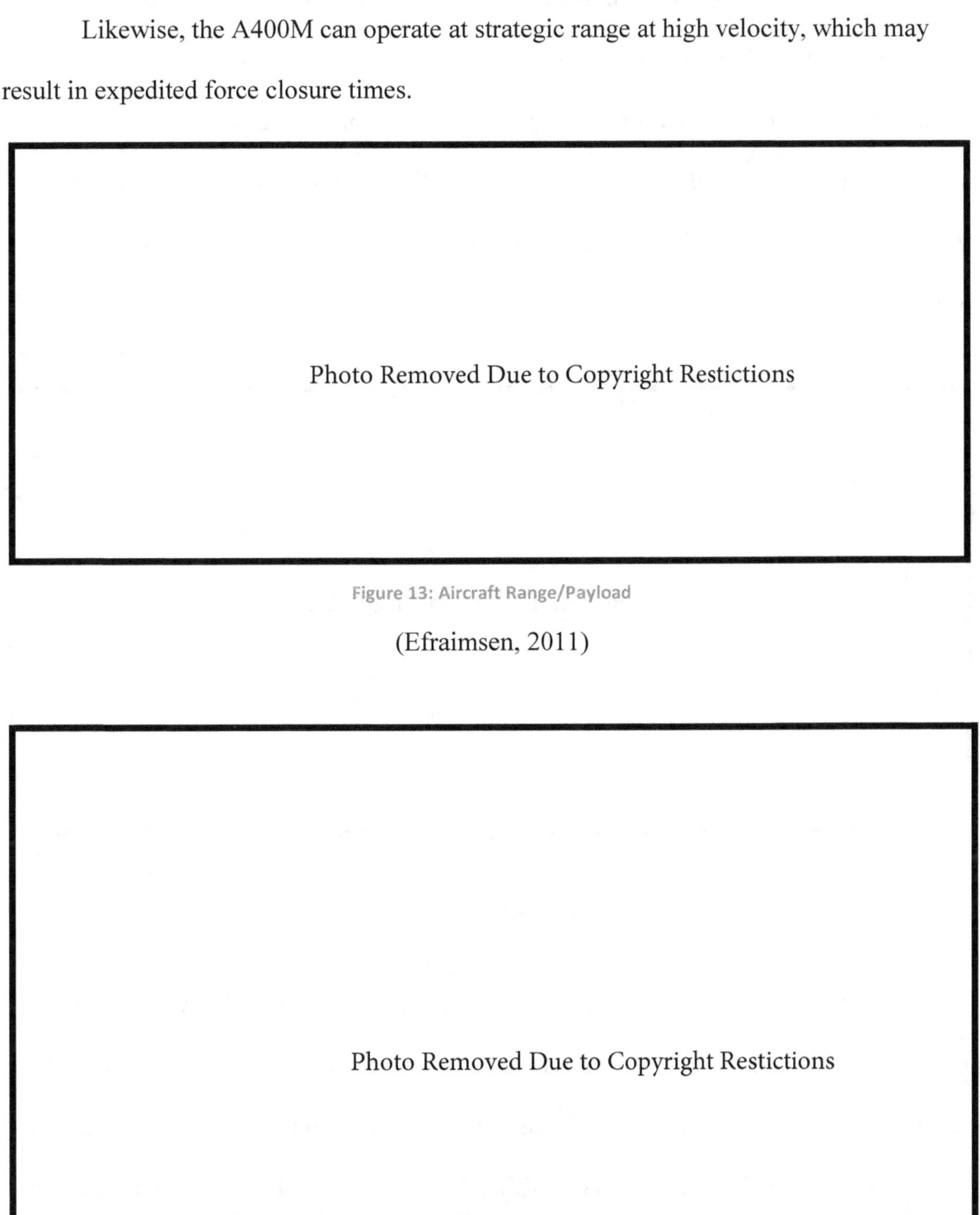

Figure 13: Aircraft Range/Payload

(Efraimsen, 2011)

Figure 14: A400M Range Map

(A400M, 2012)

The A400M project began in 1982 though the Future International Military Airlifter group. Since its initial development there have been extensive delays in delivering an operational product. The first setback was the fall of the Soviet Union, and the shift in requirements. Numerous other financial, political and engineering delays have eroded orders for the aircraft which was initially set at 291(European Defence Agency, 2011: 197). The current order includes 170 aircraft to European customers with deliveries set for Spring, 2013.

Photo Removed Due to Copyright Restictions

Figure 15: A400M Orders

(A400M, 2012)

Past studies including the 2005 JPACC study failed to include the A400M in their simulations, but did indicate that its introduction to the European fleet would substantially enhance their strategic and tactical airlift capabilities. Other studies however, indicate that the A400M will be helpful but fall short of filling the airlift gap. The Center for Strategic and International Studies indicated that, "Although the A400M will certainly provide Europe with more modern airlift capacity, it does not have the range or capacity to be considered truly strategic" (Flournoy, 2005: 87). Interviews with leading EADS representative however indicate the A400M was no intended to be a strategic lifter, but a tactical airlift platform, capable of transporting outsize cargo at strategic distance, at near jet speeds (Coolidge, 2013).

All indications are that the goals outlined by EADS will be superbly met by the A400M, yet the strategic significance of the aircraft remains. The A400M has often been referred to as the answer to Europe's strategic airlift gap. The European Defense Agency, RAND, and multiple logistics scholars are just a few voicing this opinion. This research attempts to reevaluate the 2005 JAPCC NRF deployment scenarios using the future A400M fleets. Investigating how the large A400M procurement plan will affect airlift capability for these mock NRF deployments may help determine if this is an adequate solution, or simply another piece to filing the strategic airlift gap.

III. Methodology

All models are wrong, some are useful.

– George Box

Quantifying the Capability Gap

To quantify the strategic airlift gap, a few seemingly basic questions must be answered. What is the requirement, what is the current capacity and what is the delta? These first 3 questions define the strategic airlift capability gap. The next set of questions determines how effective future airlift plans fill the defined capability gap. What is the future capacity and what is the capacity of alternatives? Answering these questions provides insight into current and future capabilities and solutions.

To quantify the requirement, the researcher determined three key variables, how much needs to be transported, at what distance and under what time constraints. Additionally, the requirements were translated into Million Ton Miles per Day (MTM/D) as yet another measure,

To determine capacity of current, future and alternate airlift fleets, the researcher had to first determine the performance capabilities of each aircraft within the fleets. Once these performance parameters were established, a series of aircraft fleets could then be used in the model to determine their overall capacity. Comparing current, future and alternative aircraft groupings against the established scenario requirements established if a capability gap exists and quantified it as a shortage of X aircraft, Y days, or Z MTM/D required.

What is the Requirement?

The information gleaned from the researcher's literature review provides the requirement. The need for expeditionary forces, deployable in short time periods by airlift is established. The size of forces and required timelines have also been established using both NATO and EU declarations, and through past exercises and research. In particular two studies provided the force structure and timelines analyzed within this research. The 2005 JAPCC ADAMS model was the primary resource used to determine requirements. The JAPCC researchers had an incredible amount of NATO expertise and access allowing them to construct a very accurate and feasible set of scenarios. This research will model both scenarios used in the JAPCC study.

Additionally, a study performed by the European Aeronautic Defense and Space Company (EADS), provided a more recent scenario modeling the multinational military effort in Mali, January 2013. While the results of the EADS model are distinctly different than those run through this research model, the force requirement serves as an accurate estimation of actual forces deployed via airlift[13]. The data included European based army battalions, as well as African army battalions. The force structure data used in this Mali deployment was used to simulate a third scenario for this research. Although much smaller (nearly 1/3rd) than the forces required for the full NRFs simulated in scenario 1 and 2, this 3rd scenario does closely approximate a smaller NRF land component, the initial response portions of a large NRF or EU battle group deployment. Past studies of the Battle Groups, suggested the initial deployment phase should occur within the first 10 days (European

---

[13] Data used in the airdrop portion of the EADS study was not used for this research. That data showed a clear benefit of using A400M in airdrop operations. The EADS study made many assumptions not used in this research to include the required ground transport from larger regional airfields to the airfield closest to the warfighter. Based on airfield surveys and C-17 tech-order data, this assumption along with others were not implemented.

Defence Agency, 2011: 20). The EADS study using large C-17, A400M and C-130 fleets found force closures fluctuate between 8.9 and 11.4 days (Smith, 2013). A time period of 10 days was then chosen for scenario 3 of this study to determine airlift shortfalls. The basic requirements derived for the three scenarios used in this research are seen in Table 12.

Table 10: Scenario Requirements

Requirements				
Scenario	Cargo (s/Tons)	Personnel	Distance (NM)	Deploy (Days)
1. Bahamas*	77,000	25,000	4,267	30
2. Rwanda	93,000	20,000	3,297	30
3. Mali (consisted of 6 battalions transported from 4 locations)				
3a. Eur Battalion x3	22,577	5,400	2,025	10
3b. Afr Battalion x1	2,004	900	1,015	10
3c. Afr Battalion x1	2,004	900	856	10
3d. Afr Battalion x1	2,004	900	541	10

*This research used Lajes AB as an enroute fuel stop for the Bahamas scenario, just as the JAPCC 2005 study did. The researcher did run models with and without the Enroute stop. Using the stop Enroute to the APOD/FOB with a direct flight overflying Lajes back to the APOE resulted in significantly shorter force closure times. This routing was within aircraft capabilities, and therefore used to maximize through-put.

Outsize Cargo

Yet another parameter used to determine requirements was the % of cargo that was outsized. The capability to carry outsized cargo was significant in the determination of cargo that could not be carried by certain aircraft in each scenario's airlift fleet. This research allowed outsize cargo to be carried on C-5, C-17, A400M and AN-124 aircraft.

For the purposes of this research, the AFPAM 10-1403 definition for outsize cargo was used: "Cargo which exceeds the dimensions 1,090''L x 117''W x 105''H. For the Mali scenario, the provided Time Phased Force and Deployment Data (TPFDD) specified what cargo met these characteristics. For the Bahamas and Rwanda scenarios, the % of outsize cargo was estimated. The estimate was based of finding from past NATO NRF deployments which found approximately 60% of airlifted cargo outsize (Massai, 2005).

62

Photo Removed Due to Copyright Restictions

Performance Capability of Aircraft

Capability data for each of the aircraft simulated was found using a number of sources. Once the capability values of the current fleet were determined for each aircraft, they were loaded into the derived equations and AMPCALC to determine their capacity. Below are a few of these resources.

AMPCALC Model

The AMPCALC model itself was provided to the researcher pre-loaded with the attributes, performance and capacity data of many aircraft. For a majority of aircraft this data was used. Aircraft not in AMPCALC, were added to the database by using published performance data provided by the manufacturers to the maximum extent. Performance values from Airbus and EADS for example were used to develop models for the AMPCALC database. This was required for some aircraft in current inventories such as the A-310 and for aircraft projected for future airlift fleets like the A400M. For example, data for A400M payload-range charts were obtained from EADS brochures, briefings and the company's online resources. That data was then used to build a scatterplot of data points.

Against the scatterplot, a linear trend line was created. The linear equation for the trend line is the input format accepted by AMPCALC to payload-range capabilities of modeled aircraft.

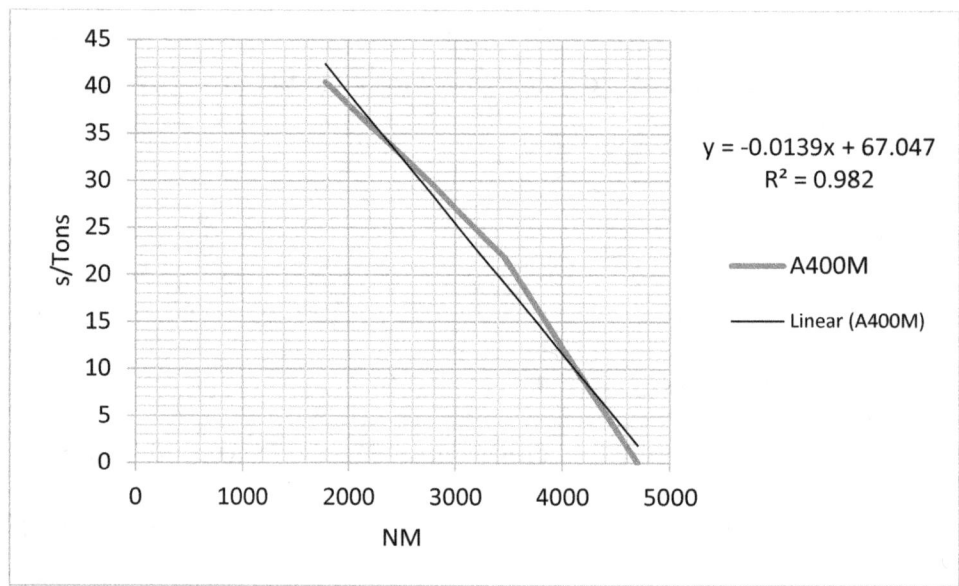

Figure 16: A400M Range-Payload inputs for AMPCALC

As seen in Figure 14 below, range-payload values were determined in this manner for the following aircraft: A400M, C-130J, VC-10, A-310, A-330, A-340. The average R^2 value for these aircraft was 0.92588, with the least corresponding to the C-130J at 0.7188[14].

---

[14] VC-10 R^2 values were omitted from these averages as the researcher had limited payload-range performance numbers that produced the VC-10 R^2 value of 1.0. The linear VC-10 values were still used in the model, as the linear payload-range error relative to the limited VC-10 had little impact on the overall results and findings.

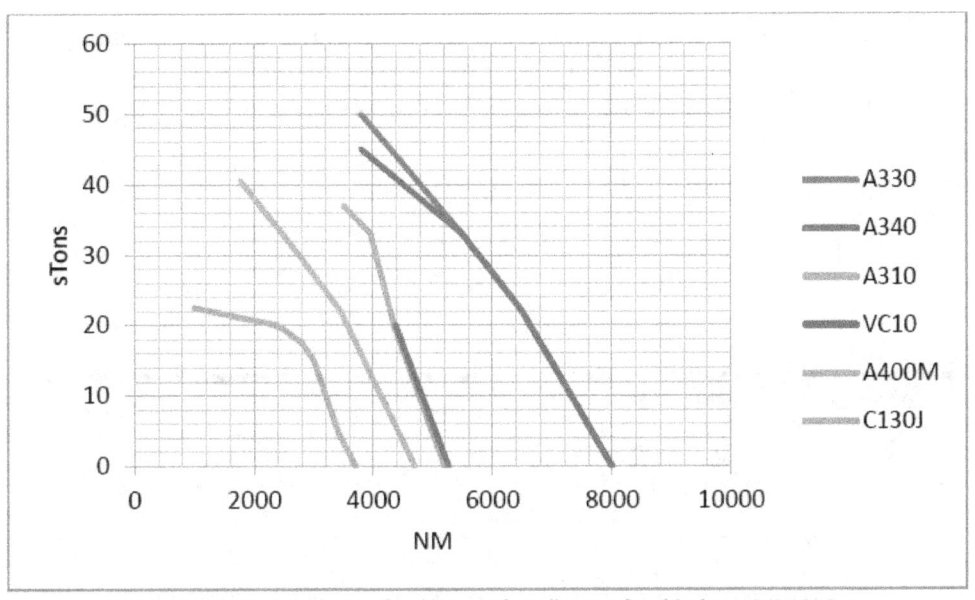

Figure 17: Range-Payload inputs for all aircraft added to AMPCALC

While the researcher does believe the method used accurately models aircraft capability, this is a recognized weakness of the model. Having non-linear payload-range data with significantly more data points of reference would benefit model accuracy.

AFPAM 10-1403

Air Force Pamphlet 10-1403: Air Mobility Planning Factors, provides air mobility planning factors for operations. It is designed to aid planners in making estimates of air mobility requirements. Aircraft block speeds, planned payloads, ground times and utilization rates were found in this pamphlet. Where data was not found for particular aircraft, estimations were made. For example, the A400M does not appear in AFPAM 10-1403, so the values were approximated through interpolation of the existing data, or given the same values of the C-17 which this research most closely compares it to. For example ground times were applied to the A400M which does not appear in AFPAM 10-1403. Enroute time were simply given the same values as the C-17, while onload/offload times

were placed between that of a C-130 and a C-17 corresponding to cargo capacity measures.
Block speed is a good example of further interpolation. Block speed is the average true
airspeed over a specified distance, including takeoff, climb, cruise, descent, approach,
landing, and taxi to block-in.

Table 12: AFPAM 10-1403 Block Speeds

Type	Mach	500nm	1000nm	1500nm	2000nm	2500nm	3000nm	3500nm	4000nm	4500nm	5000nm	5500nm	6000nm
C-130	0.49	242	266	272	273	272	271	-	-	-	-	-	-
C-130J	0.59	286	294	301	308	314	320	-	-	-	-	-	-
C-17	0.76	335	384	400	405	406	406	409	412	-	-	-	-
C-5	0.77	341	393	410	415	416	416	420	422	424	426	428	429
KC-10	0.81	354	410	428	435	436	437	440	443	446	447	449	450
KC-135	0.79	348	401	419	425	426	426	430	433	435	437	438	439
A-330	0.86	345	357	375	394	412	427	433	-	-	-	-	-
B-747	0.84	363	422	442	450	451	452	456	459	461	463	465	466
B-767	0.81	354	410	428	435	436	437	440	443	446	447	-	-
B-777	0.84	365	424	445	450	454	458	460	462	463	464	465	466
DC-8	0.80	351	405	424	430	431	432	435	438	440	442	-	-
DC-10	0.83	360	418	438	445	446	447	451	454	456	458	-	-
MD-11	0.83	360	418	438	445	446	447	451	454	456	458	460	461
Assumes standard day, pressure, temperature, -2 degree temperature lapse per 1000 feet of altitude													
Assumes 500nm leg flown at FL180 with linear increase in altitude to FL450 for 4000nm and beyond													
Assumes 20 minute airborne delay for departure, approach, and landing													
Assumes 5 minute taxi time from landing to block in													
Total time measured from rotation on takeoff leg to block-in after landing													
Total distance measured from point of takeoff to point of landing													
Changes in planned cruise airspeed will alter results													

NOTE: Organic aircraft block speeds obtained from computer flight plan data. Civil aircraft figures are a composite average of various configurations and series participating in CRAF. For Civil aircraft whose passenger and cargo configuration speeds differed, the lower speed was used. All airspeeds are TAS.

Using data provided by EADS, the A400M's cruising speed was found to be very close to
the average of C-130J and KC-10 speeds, giving the turboprop jet like speeds. Using this
average speed distribution and interpolating the block speed table provided by AFPAM 10-
1403 (above), the following block speeds were calculated and input into AMPCALC.

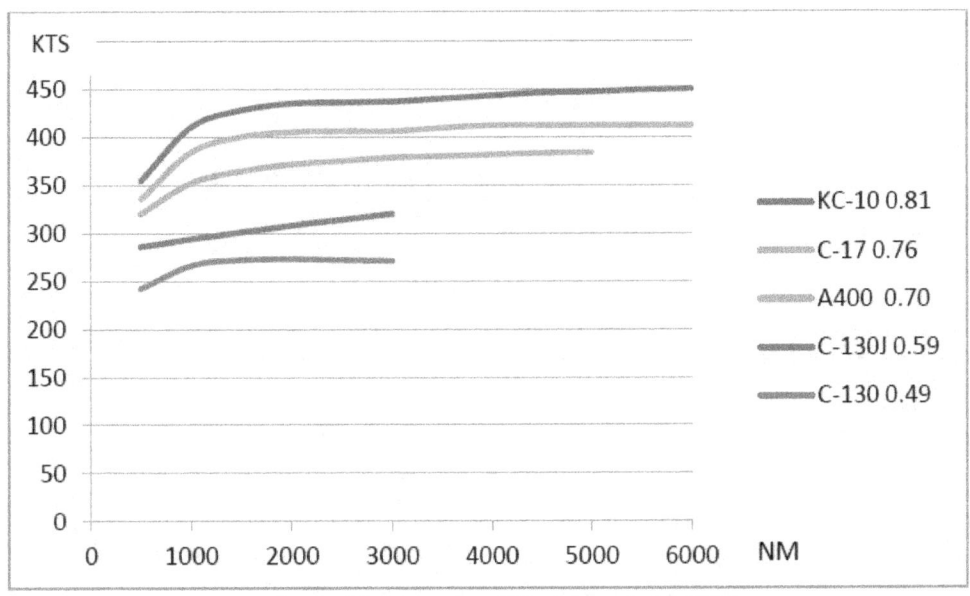

Figure 18: Interpolated Block Speed of A400M

Million Ton Miles per Day (MTM/D)

Million Ton Miles per Day (MTM/D) is a metric used in the transportation industry to measure a logistic requirement or fleet capacity. "AMC force structure programmers use MTM/D when funding out-year aircraft purchases and many civilian agencies are accustomed to visualizing our fleet capability in terms of MTM/D" (AFPAM 10-1403, 2011: 4). There are two variations of calculating MTM/D. The first determines the MTM/D capability of a given fleet of aircraft.

$$MTM/D = \# \ Aircraft \times Avg \ Payload \times Block \ Speed \times Ute \ Rate \times Productivity \ Factor$$

Equation 1: MTM/D (Aircraft Perspective)

Equation 1 was used after a fleet size was determined by AMPCALC running the scenarios. These values are discussed further in the results section of this study.

The second variation of MTM/D, takes a cargo perspective, as it determines the MTM/D required to move a finite requirement a given distance within a specific time

67

period.

$$MTM/D = \frac{(Tons\ Delivered \times Miles\ Flown)}{(Days\ Required \times 1,000,000)}$$

Equation 2: MTM/D (Cargo Perspective)

Equations 2 provides a baseline for determining what the requirements are for each scenario and are displayed in Table 15.

Table 13: Scenario MTM/D (Cargo Requirements)

Scenario MTM/D (Cargo Requirements)				
Scenario	Cargo (s/Tons)	Distance (NM)	Deploy (Days)	MTM/D
1. Bahamas	77,000	4,267	30	10.952
2. Rwanda	93,000	3,297	30	10.165
3. Mali (consisted of 6 Battalions transported from 4 locations)				
3a. Eur Battalion x3	22,577	2,025	10	4.572
3b. Afr Battalion x1	2,004	1,015	10	0.203
3c. Afr Battalion x1	2,004	856	10	0.172
3d. Afr Battalion x1	2,004	541	10	0.108

MTM/D for Scenarios 1-3 (including each segment of Mali deployment)

Airlift Fleets

The capacity for Europe's current strategic airlift fleet was determined by examining actual aircraft fleets and determining their capability within each scenario. The primary source for airlift fleet sizes was the JAPCC's 2011 "NATO Air Transport Capability- An Assessment." Numbers of aircraft, variants and owning nations were quantified in this document. Much of the information obtained from this JPACC document can be found in Annex A. Not all available aircraft were used for this study, as the scenarios were built to purposefully test strategic capabilities. Tactical aircraft such as the C-160 and C-27J were not included in the models. This research centered on European strategic airlift, and as such, omitted U.S. and Canadian aircraft from the study as well. The "Current" fleet was

composed of the following:

Table 14: "Current" Strategic Airlift Fleet

"Current" Strategic Airlift Fleet	
Aircraft	Total (Europe)
C17	10
A310	10
A330	14
A340	2
KDC10	3
KC767	2
C130J	62
C130H	107
AN124	4*

The fleet described in Table 16 above was used in total for the Bahamas and

Rwanda Scenarios. The Mali Scenario cargo was limited to C-17, C-130 and A400M

aircraft due to airfield restrictions. The SALIS contract guarantees 6 AN-124s, but they are

limited to 20 days or 800hrs per month. Mirroring the 2005 JAPCC study, the researcher

limited the AN-124 fleet using the 20 day per month constraint which approximates 66% of

full fleet use per month, or 4 AN-124 aircraft. To account for the "assured" access to the

aircraft, the maintenance capability rate for the AN-124s modeled was kept at 100% rather

than the 85% used for the rest of the fleet.

Future airlift fleets were examined by projecting current procurement initiatives to

fruition and eliminating aircraft being currently phased out. Results included the addition

of 170 A400Ms and the removal of all VC-10[15]. In addition, the AN-124s provided by

---

[15] At the onset of this research the VC-10 was still in the inventory in limited numbers and use. The researcher acknowledges that the VC-10 has since been decommissioned and has removed it from the

SALIS were taken away in response to publically stated intentions to do so once the A400Ms were operational. The "Future" airlift fleet was composed of the following:

Table 15: "Future" Strategic Airlift Fleet

"Future" Strategic Airlift Fleet	
Aircraft	Total (Europe)
C17	10
A400	170
A310	10
A330	14
A340	4
KDC10	3
KC767	4
C130J	70
C130H	107

The above fleet was used in total for the Bahamas and Rwanda Scenarios. The Mali Scenario cargo was limited to C-17, C-130 and A400M aircraft due to airfield restrictions.

The future fleet in table 17 was used in total for the Bahamas and Rwanda Scenarios. The Mali scenario was limited to C-17, C-130 and A400M aircraft due to airfield restrictions.

The alternate airlift fleet simply looked at the capacity possible if European allies had decided to expand their fleet of C-17 aircraft rather than purchase the A400M. This fleet was manipulated to determine how many were needed to meet requirements, and how many were needed to match projected A400M fleet performance. AMCALC is able to isolate the amount of cargo transported by each aircraft type in an assigned fleet for each scenario.

Determining Current Capacity

To answer each of the fundamental questions defining a possible capability gap,

---

"Current Fleet". The inclusion of the VC-10 did however prove useful in the running of JAPCC's NRF deployment scenario using 2005 fleets for AMPCALC scenario validation.

multiple models were run. The first set of models examined the current fleet of European strategic airlifters and their performance within each of the three scenarios. These models first determined how many days it would take to deliver the required cargo to the given destination. The models were then run again to see how much cargo the fleet was capable of transporting within the specified time constraint (i.e. 30 days). MTM/D for the fleet (Equation 2) was also calculated and compared to the MTM/D required (Equation 1) for each scenario.

Scenario 1 (Bahamas)

Model CurB-1: Current Fleet to Bahamas (moving all cargo)

Model CurB-2: Current Fleet to Bahamas (constrained to 30 days)

Scenario 2 (Rwanda)

Model CurR-1: Current Fleet to Rwanda (moving all cargo)

Model CurR-2: Current Fleet to Rwanda (constrained to 30 days)

Scenario 3 (Mali)

Model CurM-1: Current Fleet* to Mali (moving all cargo)

Model CurM-2: Current Fleet* to Mali (constrained to 10 days)

The Mali Scenario cargo was limited to C-17, C-130 and A400M aircraft due to airfield restrictions.

Determining Future Capacity

The second set of models updated the fleet with aircraft as described in Table 17. As with the Current fleet, these models first determined how many days it would take to deliver the required cargo to the specified destination. The models were then run again to see how much cargo the fleet was capable of transporting within the specified time constraint (i.e. 30 days). MTM/D for the fleet (Equation 2) was also calculated and compared to the MTM/D required (Equation 1) for the scenario.

Scenario 1 (Bahamas)

Model FutB-1: Future Fleet to Bahamas (moving all cargo)

Model FutB-2: Future Fleet to Bahamas (constrained to 30 days)

Scenario 2 (Rwanda)

Model FutR-1: Future Fleet to Rwanda (moving all cargo)

Model FutR-2: Future Fleet to Rwanda (constrained to 30 days)

Scenario 3 (Mali)

Model FutM-1: Future Fleet* to Mali (moving all cargo)

Model FutM-2: Future Fleet* to Mali (constrained to 10 days)

> * *The Mali Scenario cargo was limited to C-17, C-130 and A400M aircraft due to airfield restrictions.*

Determining Alternate Capacity

A third set of model runs sought to determine how an expanded European fleet of C-17s would compare to the proposed addition of A400Ms. A possible expansion of SAC or simply reallocation of money from A400M investments makes this hypothetical fleet feasible. Not knowing exactly how many C-17s may hypothetically be added to a future fleet drove the researcher to devise additional model runs. As part of the alternate fleet capacity determination, additional runs were completed to isolate A400M and C-17 allocated cargo from the time constrained model runs (FutB-2 & FutR-2). With the required A400Ms established from Models FutB-2 & Fut R-2, these models were then run substituting C-17s for A400Ms to determine the corresponding number of required C-17s to meet a 30 day force closure.

Scenario 1 (Bahamas)

Model AltB-2: Alternate Fleet to Bahamas (constrained to 30 days)

<u>Scenario 2 (Rwanda)</u>

Model AltR-2: Alternate Fleet to Rwanda (constrained to 30 days)

Algebraic Validation

Finally, algebraic equations listed in AFPAM 10-1403 and further defined in *The Algebra of Airlift* article, were used to validate alternate fleet results determined by the AMPCALC model runs. These equations are actually the basis for the AMPCALC deterministic model, so when isolated without the additional refining variables of AMPCALC, gross solutions to the airlift gap questions are presented. Comparing the results between the simplified equations and more the comprehensive model show that results were fairly close to one another. Each of the variables and equations were built into a spreadsheet calculator which can be seen below.

$$Number\ of\ Cargo\ Missions = \frac{Cargo\ Requirement}{Average\ Payload}$$

Equation 3: Number of Cargo Missions

$$Round\ Trip\ Flying\ Time, RTFT = (Leg\ Dist_1 / Block\ Speed_1) + (Leg\ Dist_2 / Block\ Speed_2) + \ldots + (Leg\ Dist_n / Block\ Speed_n)[\text{hrs}]$$

Equation 4: Rount Trip Flying Time

$$Average\ Block\ Speed = \frac{Round\ Trip\ Distance}{RTFT}[\text{nm/hr}]$$

Equation 5: Average Block Speed

$$Total\ Ground\ Time, TGT = Onload\ Time + \{(Enroute\ Time) \times (Number\ of\ Enroute\ Stops\ in\ Cycle)\} + Offload\ Time\ [\text{hrs}]$$

Equation 6: Total Ground Time

$$Cycle\ Time = RTFT + TGT\ [\text{hrs}]$$

Equation 7: Cycle Time

$$Station\ Interval = \frac{Station\ Ground\ Time}{Station\ Capability}\ [\text{hrs}]$$

Equation 8: Station Interval

$$PMAI\ Allocation = TAI - BAI - TF$$

Equation 9: PMAI Allocation

$$Aircraft\ Allocation\ Interval = \frac{Cycle\ Time}{PMAI\ Allocation}\ [\text{hrs}]$$

Equation 10: Aircraft Allocation Interval

$$Scenario\ Use\ Rate = \frac{Scenario\ Flying\ Time \times 24}{Scenario\ Flying\ Time + Planned\ Ground\ Time}\ [\text{hrs/day}]$$

Equation 11: Scenario Use Rate

$$Objective\ Ute\ Rate = \frac{(PMAI\ Allocation \times MC\ Rate - JCS\ Withholds) \times Scenario\ Use\ Rate + (JCS\ Withholds \times 4)}{PMAI\ Allocation}\ [\text{hrs/day}]$$

Equation 12: Objective Ute Rate

$$Flying\ Hour\ Capability\ Interval = \frac{RTFT \times 24}{Objective\ Ute\ Rate \times PMAI\ Allocation}\ [\text{hrs}]$$

Equation 13: Flying Hour Capability Interval

$$Flow\ Interval = \max\{StationInterval,\ AircraftInterval,\ FlyingHourCapabilityInterval\}\ [\text{hrs}]$$

16

Equation 14: Flow Interval

$$Closure = \frac{(Missions\ Required - 1) \times (Flow\ Interval) + One\ Way\ Enroute\ Time}{24}\ [\text{days}]$$

Equation 15: Closure

$$Prime\ Aircraft\ Required = \frac{Cycle\ Time}{Flow\ Interval}$$

Equation 16: Prime Aircraft Required

$$Tons\ per\ Day = \frac{Average\ Payload \times 24 \times Prime\ Aircraft\ Required}{Cycle\ Time}\ [\text{STons/D}]$$

Equation 17: Tons per Day

$$Ute\ Rate = \frac{RTFT \times 24}{Flow\ Interval \times PMAI\ Allocation}\ [\text{hrs/day}]$$

Equation 18: Ute Rate

---

[16] Stage Crew Interval should also be included, however this research assumed no crew constraints. Similarly, models were run without station interval constraints. MOG levels were simulated to unconstrained levels.

$$Actual\ Productivity\ Factor = \frac{One\,Way\ En\ Route\ Flying\ Time}{RTFT + Origin\,to\ Onload\ Flying\ Time}$$

$$Million\ Ton\,Miles\ per\ Day = Average\,Block\ Speed \times Ute\ Rate \times Productivity\ Factor \times$$
$$Average\,Payload \times PMAI\ Allocation\ /1{,}000{,}000\ [MTMs/D]$$

Assumptions

As with any model this study's included many inaccuracies. The simplified rendering of real-world scenarios was limited to finite data with many assumptions and limitations. Below are some of the more significant assumptions used to simplify this research.

1) 100% access to European airlift

   - The NRF Commander has 100% access to European fleet of aircraft. It is unlikely that all nations would offer 100% of their airlift to any given contingency, however this assumption allowed the researcher to test the full capabilities of the European airlift inventory.

2) Pooling agreements remain in effect

   - Aircraft sourced from multinational initiatives such as SAC and SALIS remain available.

3) Deployable forces ready for movement as airlift is available

   - This assumption removes any delays that may be caused by unit readiness or prepositioning.

4) Cargo always available to max load aircraft

76

5) U.S. enroute support available for scenarios

  - Scenario 1 uses Lajes AB as an Enroute stop.

6) Air to Air refueling not used

7) Stable/accurate Ute rates

  - Over the course of a month –long deployment, utilization rates may fluctuate. For the purposes of this study, they remain constant.

8) CRAF-like support not available

  - Civilian cargo airlift is not used in any scenario to test the capability of the European organic airlift fleet. One exception is the chartered AN-124s via SALIS.

9) AN-124 Limited to 20 days / 800 hours

  - This matches the contract constraints that were used in the 2005 JAPCC study

10) SALIS remains temporary

  - For the composition of the "Future" fleet, SALIS AN-124s are removed as planned with the delivery of A400Ms.

11) Multimodal support not used

  - This study examines only the force requirements feasibly transported by airlift only.

12) NRF will rely on airlift to meet acceptable deployment times via direct delivery to the area of operation.

13) Requirements are conflict based

- Deployed forces are based on European combat units. All lift attempts to deliver forces at the AOR, mitigating the use of near-by airfields which would require further ground-transport for warfighter delivery.

14) AOR and enroute structure threat-free

- No aircraft losses or damage occur throughout the deployment scenarios.

15) 95% aircraft availability

- 5% of all aircraft are considered unavailable due to training, depot maintenance or other unavailability. This is an optimistic figure as U.S. C-17 fleets typically have 8% unavailable for operations due to training alone (Leshiker, 2006)

16) 85% mission capability rate

- This assumption mirrors the 2005 JAPCC study which used a maintenance break rate of 15%.

17) Airflow is not affected by onward movement restrictions.

- Maximum on Ground (MOG) is not constraining. This assumption avoids testing the Enroute structure, allowing focus on fleet potential. The assumption is one that may particularly skew the future fleet with such a large fleet of A400M aircraft participating with numerous C-130s.

18) Unlimited storage space at the APOE

- Offload capabilities are not hampered by the models frequent arrivals, thus working MOG is not affected.

19) Crew availability not a limiting factor

- This assumption avoids testing the crew force requirements, allowing focus on fleet potential. This assumption is one that may particularly skew the future fleet with such a large fleet of A400M aircraft participating with numerous C-130s. The researcher recognizes that significant crew staging would be necessary to operate as modeled. Cycle times some model scenarios exceed 24 hours.

20) C-17, A400M and C-130 capable of direct delivery

- These aircraft are able to fly in and out of all simulated airfields. Fields selected in Mali were the most restrictive and preclude the use of all MRTT aircraft, yet meet all minimum takeoff and landing criteria for these aircraft.

21) MRTT aircraft always maximized for passenger movement prior to cargo use.

- Once all passengers moved, MRTT aircraft are then used for cargo movement of bulk cargo only.

22) Aircraft do not cube-out

- Aircraft performance is restricted only by cargo weight, not cargo volume.

Limitations

Any model used is simply a limited interpretation of the real-world and as such will suffer from limitations in simulating reality. Along with the inherent limitations that each of the assumptions above contribute, the following limits were placed on this study to control its scope and focus.

1) All forces are deployed from a single European location.

- In reality forces would likely be flown to the APOD from multiple APOE across Europe. This model used the central location of Ramstein AB has its single APOE.

2) Consolidation of forces is not considered

- In using a single APOE, forces would need to be consolidated there for strategic transport to the final APOD. The airlift assets and time required to consolidate forces at the strategic staging base is not considered in this study. In reality the fleets used for this study would suffer attrition as aircraft would be needed for intra-theater lift within Europe for force consolidation.

3) Crew availability not a limiting factor

- This assumption avoids testing crew force requirements, allowing focus on fleet potential. This assumption is one that may particularly skew the future fleet with such a large fleet of A400M aircraft participating with numerous C-130s. The researcher recognizes that significant crew staging would be necessary to operate as modeled. Cycle times some model scenarios exceed 24 hours.

4) Tactical aircraft not modeled

- Small tactical aircraft with short ranges and light payloads were not included in this study. In reality large numbers of these aircraft could theoretically have a small but significant impact on findings.

5) Effects of air to air refueling not included

6) Effect of MOG not included

7) Effects of crew ratios not included

IV. Results and Analysis

The three scenarios were first examined by calculating the MTM/D required to move all requirements in the specified time using Equation 2. These values are listed for each scenario on the last column of the scenario requirements tables below. These values served as a baseline to determine the gap between requirements and fleet capability.

Next, each set of models examined the current, future and alternate fleets of European strategic airlifters and their performance within each of the three scenarios. These models first determined how many days it would take to deliver the required cargo to the given destination. The models were then run again to see how much cargo the current fleet was capable of transporting within the specified time constraint (i.e. 30 days). Models were also run for each scenario deleting MRTT aircraft as viable cargo carriers to simulate the added constraint of inadequate airfields. These results although not shown in total are discussed within each scenario analysis as appropriate. The tables below display only a fraction of the data produced by AMCALC, but represent the most pertinent information for this study. The information shaded gray are inputs, those in white are outputs.

Scenario 1: Bahamas

Table 16: Scenario 1 Requirements

Scenario Requirements				
Scenario	Cargo (s/Tons)	Distance (NM)	Deploy (Days)	MTM/D
1. Bahamas	77,000	4,267	30	10.952

Current Capacity

Scenario 1: Bahamas w/Current Fleet (64.79 Days to Move All Requirements)												
Results	Closure =	64.79										
Aircraft Type	# Acft Cargo	# Acft Pax	Outsize Tons	Bulk Tons	Total Tons	Cargo Missions	Pax Missions	Total Missions	Average Payload	MTM per Day	Tons per Day	Passengers per Day
AN124	4	0	18,547.2	5,480.6	24,027.8	148	0	148	125.89	1.24	286	0
A310	9	10	0.0	3,600.2	3,600.2	244	31	275	37.00	0.81	187	1,148
KC-10	3	0	0.0	633.8	633.8	49	0	49	32.60	0.14	33	0
KC767	1	2	0.0	0.0	0.0	0	4	4	33.00	0.00	0	163
C130H	107	0	0.0	2,848.9	2,848.9	832	0	832	8.56	0.64	148	0
C130J	62	0	0.0	3,115.1	3,115.1	557	0	557	14.00	0.70	162	0
A340	1	2	0.0	0.0	0.0	0	4	4	45.00	0.00	0	305
A330	12	14	0.0	6,950.1	6,950.1	348	42	390	50.00	1.57	361	2,772
C17	10	0	27,652.8	8,171.3	35,824.1	363	0	363	76.26	1.84	427	0
Total	209	28	46,200.0	30,800.0	77,000.0	2,541	81	2,622	0.00	6.94	1,604	4,387

Significant Results:

1. *Current Fleet closure of 64.79 well above 30 day goal*

2. *Capable of moving only 6.94 of required 10.95 MTM/D*

Scenario 1: Bahamas w/Current Fleet (47.7k sTons Moved in 30 Days)												
Results	Closure =	30.28										
Aircraft Type	# Acft Cargo	# Acft Pax	Outsize Tons	Bulk Tons	Total Tons	Cargo Missions	Pax Missions	Total Missions	Average Payload	MTM per Day	Tons per Day	Passengers per Day
AN124	4	0	8,510.8	4,715.5	13,226.3	68	0	68	125.89	1.24	284	0
A310	9	10	0.0	3,097.5	3,097.5	151	31	182	37.00	0.81	186	1,148
KC-10	3	0	0.0	545.3	545.3	31	0	31	32.60	0.14	33	0
KC767	1	2	0.0	0.0	0.0	0	4	4	33.00	0.00	0	163
C130H	107	0	0.0	2,451.1	2,451.1	516	0	516	8.56	0.64	146	0
C130J	62	0	0.0	2,680.2	2,680.2	345	0	345	14.00	0.70	160	0
A340	1	2	0.0	0.0	0.0	0	4	4	45.00	0.00	0	305
A330	12	14	0.0	5,979.8	5,979.8	216	42	258	50.00	1.57	357	2,772
C17	10	0	12,689.2	7,030.5	19,719.7	167	0	167	76.26	1.84	421	0
Total	209	28	21,200.0	26,500.0	47,700.0	1,494	81	1,575	0.00	6.94	1,586	4,387

Significant Results:

1. *Current Fleet can only move 61% of required cargo in 30 days.*

Future Capacity

Table 19: Model FutB-1

Scenario 1: Bahamas w/Future Fleet (20.95 Days to Move All Requirements)												
Results	Closure =	20.95										
Aircraft Type	# Acft Cargo	# Acft Pax	Outsize Tons	Bulk Tons	Total Tons	Cargo Missions	Pax Missions	Total Missions	Average Payload	MTM per Day	Tons per Day	Passengers per Day
A310	7	10	0.0	1,085.4	1,085.4	74	26	100	37.00	0.58	131	1,124
KC-10	3	0	0.0	267.5	267.5	21	0	21	32.60	0.14	33	0
KC767	3	4	0.0	387.2	387.2	30	10	40	33.00	0.21	47	407
C130H	107	0	0.0	1,202.5	1,202.5	352	0	352	8.56	0.64	144	0
C130J	70	0	0.0	1,491.8	1,491.8	267	0	267	14.00	0.80	179	0
A340	2	4	0.0	264.0	264.0	15	10	25	45.00	0.14	33	762
A330	10	14	0.0	2,346.8	2,346.8	118	36	154	50.00	1.25	283	2,717
C17	10	0	6,707.9	3,449.0	10,156.9	114	0	114	76.26	1.84	415	0
A400M	170	0	39,492.1	20,305.7	59,797.8	1,687	0	1,687	30.09	10.84	2,433	0
Total	382	32	46,200.0	30,800.0	77,000.0	2,678	82	2,760	0.00	16.45	3,696	5,010

Significant Results:

    1. Future Fleet closure of 20.95 days well below 30 day goal.

Table 20: Model FutB-2

Scenario 1: Bahamas w/Future Fleet (77k sTons Moved in 30 Days)												
Results	Closure =	30.16										
Aircraft Type	# Acft Cargo	# Acft Pax	Outsize Tons	Bulk Tons	Total Tons	Cargo Missions	Pax Missions	Total Missions	Average Payload	MTM per Day	Tons per Day	Passengers per Day
A310	7	10	0.0	1,586.6	1,586.6	108	26	134	37.00	0.58	132	1,124
KC-10	3	0	0.0	391.1	391.1	30	0	30	32.60	0.14	34	0
KC767	3	4	0.0	566.0	566.0	43	10	53	33.00	0.21	48	407
C130H	107	0	0.0	1,757.7	1,757.7	514	0	514	8.56	0.64	146	0
C130J	70	0	0.0	2,180.7	2,180.7	390	0	390	14.00	0.80	181	0
A340	2	4	0.0	385.9	385.9	22	10	32	45.00	0.14	33	762
A330	10	14	0.0	3,430.6	3,430.6	172	36	208	50.00	1.25	286	2,717
C17	10	0	11,361.5	5,041.7	16,403.2	166	0	166	76.26	1.84	420	0
A400M	89	0	34,838.5	15,459.6	50,298.1	1,285	0	1,285	30.09	5.65	1,284	0
Total	301	32	46,200.0	30,800.0	77,000.0	2,730	82	2,812	0.00	11.25	2,565	5,010

Significant Results:

    1. Only 89 of projected 170 A400Ms required to complete full closure in 30 days.

Alternate Capacity

A third set of model runs sought to determine how an expanded European fleet of

C-17s would compare to the proposed addition of A400Ms. The researcher isolated

A400M and C-17 allocated cargo from the time constrained model runs (FutB-2 & FutR-2).

With the required A400Ms established from Models FutB-2 & Fut R-2, these models were

then run substituting C-17s for A400Ms to determine the corresponding number of required

C-17s to meet a 30 day force closure

83

Results	Closure =	30.45											
				Scenario 1: Bahamas w/Alternate Fleet (77k sTons Moved in 30 Days)									
Aircraft Type	# Acft Cargo	# Acft Pax	Outsize Tons	Bulk Tons	Total Tons	Cargo Missions	Pax Missions	Total Missions	Average Payload	MTM per Day	Tons per Day	Passengers per Day
A310	7	10	0.0	1,604.1	1,604.1	109	26	135	37.00	0.58	133	1,124
KC-10	3	0	0.0	395.3	395.3	31	0	31	32.60	0.14	33	0
KC767	3	4	0.0	572.3	572.3	44	10	54	33.00	0.21	48	407
C130H	107	0	0.0	1,777.1	1,777.1	519	0	519	8.56	0.64	146	0
C130J	70	0	0.0	2,204.7	2,204.7	394	0	394	14.00	0.80	181	0
A340	2	4	0.0	390.2	390.2	22	10	32	45.00	0.14	33	762
A330	10	14	0.0	3,468.2	3,468.2	174	36	210	50.00	1.25	286	2,717
C17	38	0	46,200.0	20,388.2	66,588.2	669	0	669	76.26	7.37	1,680	0
Total	240	32	46,200.0	30,800.0	77,000.0	1,962	82	2,044	0.00	11.13	2,540	5,010

Significant Results:

1. Only 38 C-17s required to complete closure in 30 days. (28 added to current

fleet)

Algebraic Validation

Algebraic equations listed in AFPAM 10-1403 and further defined in *The Algebra*

of Airlift article, were used to validate alternate fleet results determined by the AMPCALC

model runs. These equations are actually the basis for the AMPCALC deterministic model,

so when isolated without the additional refining variables of AMPCALC, gross solutions to

the airlift gap questions are presented. Comparing the results between the simplified

equations and the more comprehensive model show fairly similar results. The equations

run to determine the fleet size required to obtain closure within 30 days. The deviation

from AMPCALC's model results (in terms of aircraft required) can be seen at the bottom of

the tables below. This method was only applied to the analysis of Scenarios 1 & 2.

Scenario 1: Bahamas C-17		Scenario 1: Bahamas A400M	
Cargo Requirement	66588.19	Cargo Requirement	50298.11
Average Payload	76.26	Average Payload	30.09
Number of Cargo Msns	873.17	Number of Cargo Msns	1671.59
Leg1 Flying Distance	1608.00	Leg1 Flying Distance	1608.00
Leg1 Block Speed	401.00	Leg1 Block Speed	366.00
Leg1 Flying Time	4.01	Leg1 Flying Time	4.39
Leg2 Flying Distance	2659.00	Leg2 Flying Distance	2659.00
Leg2 Block Speed	406.00	Leg2 Block Speed	376.00
Leg2 Flying Time	6.55	Leg2 Flying Time	7.07
Total 1 Way Fly Time	10.56	Total 1 Way Fly Time	11.47
Return Flying Distance	4089.00	Return Flying Distance	4089.00
Return Block Speed	412.00	Return Block Speed	382.00
Return Flying Time	9.92	Return Flying Time	10.70
Round Trip Flying Time	20.48	Round Trip Flying Time	22.17
Round Trip Distance	8356.00	Round Trip Distance	8356.00
Avg Block Speed	407.93	Avg Block Speed	376.92
Onload Time	4.00	Onload Time	4.00
Enroute Stop Time	2.50	Enroute Stop Time	2.50
Num of Enroute Stops	1.00	Num of Enroute Stops	1.00
Offload Times	3.25	Offload Times	2.75
Total Gnd Time	9.75	Total Gnd Time	9.25
Cycle Time	30.23	Cycle Time	31.42
Station Ground Time	2.75	Station Ground Time	2.75
Station Capability	999.00	Station Capability	999.00
Station Interval	0.00	Station Interval	0.00
Total Aircraft Inventory	47.00	Total Aircraft Inventory	95.00
Backup Aircraft Inventory	0.00	Backup Aircraft Inventory	0.00
Training Fence (5%)	2.35	Training Fence (5%)	4.75
Primary Msn Acft Inventory	44.65	Primary Msn Acft Inventory	90.25
Aircraft Allocation Interval	0.68	Aircraft Allocation Interval	0.35
MC Rate	0.85	MC Rate	0.85
Scenario Use Rate	16.26	Scenario Use Rate	16.93
Objective Ute Rate	13.18	Objective Ute Rate	13.71
Flying Hour Capability Interval	0.84	Flying Hour Capability Interval	0.43
Flow Interval	0.84	Flow Interval	0.43
Closure	30.81	Closure	30.40
Prime Aircraft Required	36.18	Prime Aircraft Required	73.08
Tons per Day	2190.22	Tons per Day	1679.81
Ute Rate	13.18	Ute Rate	13.71
Actual Productivity Factor	0.52	Actual Productivity Factor	0.52
MTM/D	9.43	MTM/D	7.26
% Deviation from AMCALC (Acft req'd for 30 day closure)	0.13	% Deviation from AMCALC (Acft req'd for 30 day closure)	0.01

Significant Results:

1. 45C-17 required vs. 38 calculated by AMCALC (12.65% Difference)

2. 90 A400M required vs. 89 calculated by AMCALC (1.39% Difference)

Scenario 1 Analysis

Scenario 1 to the Bahamas was very taxing on the European fleet. While Scenario 2 to Rwanda did include a greater amount of cargo, Scenario 1's distance of more than 8,000 miles round trip placed an enormous stress on airlift. Both MTM/D algebra and modeling concluded that a significant gap exists in Europe's current airlift fleet, yet their future fleet should have adequate capacity.

Within Scenario 1 and in all scenarios, passenger movement was never a limiting factor. Without procuring commercial transport, NATO allies have more than enough capacity to rapidly move expeditionary forces. This is of course if airfields in or near the AOR allow access to their more commercially derived aircraft. Regarding the transport of cargo, the current airlift fleet was only capable of moving 6.94 MTM/D. This includes using all MRTT aircraft for cargo when not used in their primary role of passenger transport. This falls well short of the calculated 10.95 MTM/D required. When modeled for best closure, the results show an even larger gap by a factor of 2.16. What the allies want to move in 30 days was determined to take nearly 65. When the model was limited to 30 days available the results mirrored previous findings, showing only 47.7k s/Tons of the required 77k s/Tons could be delivered (61%).

Modeling the future fleet resulted in much better results. With the most notable changes being the deletion of SALIS AN-124s and the addition of 170 A400Ms, all requirements were delivered in less than 21 days. These results of course benefit from the full use of all European strategic airlifters from all continental allies, hampered only by a

5% training fence and 15% maintenance fail rate. Although optimistic, these assumptions may not be unfeasible in an effort of grave importance to the allies as a whole.

Once the model was restricted to 30 days, the researcher was able to narrow down a more accurate number of A400Ms needed to complete the scenario. A more manageable 89 A400Ms, or only 52% of the projected total was required. Likewise, mobility based algebra resulted in 90 A400Ms required.

By substituting additional C-17s for A400Ms in an alternate future fleet, the research implied only 28 additional C-17 would offer the same force closure. Algebraic validation found 35 more C-17 would be required. With only $1/3^{rd}$ the number of C-17s required, one could speculate on the advantages of purchasing additional C-17 rather than numerously more A400Ms. The feasibility of this alternate fleet is explored more in the discussion section of this paper.

Whether looking at MTM/D, obtainable force closure timetables, or cargo capabilities within outlined timelines, scenario 1 shows a significant capability gap. This gap however is adequately bridged through the projected purchase of A400M aircraft. In fact only half of those under contract would be needed to accomplish European contingency objectives for the given scenario.

Scenario 2: Rwanda

Table 23: Scenario 2 Requirements

Scenario Requirements				
Scenario	Cargo (s/Tons)	Distance (NM)	Deploy (Days)	MTM/D
2. Rwanda	93,000	3,297	30	10.165

Current Capacity

Table 24: Model CurR-1

Results	Closure =	73.59	Scenario 2: Rwanda w/Current Fleet (73.59 Days to Move All Requirements)									
Aircraft Type	# Acft Cargo	# Acft Pax	Outsize Tons	Bulk Tons	Total Tons	Cargo Missions	Pax Missions	Total Missions	Average Payload	MTM per Day	Tons per Day	Passengers per Day
AN124	4	0	22,749.7	6,478.2	29,228.0	213	0	213	107.11	1.02	309	0
A310	9	10	0.0	5,068.2	5,068.2	343	25	368	37.00	0.80	241	1,493
KC-10	3	0	0.0	882.5	882.5	68	0	68	32.60	0.14	42	0
KC767	1	2	0.0	0.0	0.0	0	4	4	33.00	0.00	0	217
C130H	107	0	0.0	1,750.8	1,750.8	1,161	0	1,161	3.77	0.28	83	0
C130J	62	0	0.0	2,846.3	2,846.3	789	0	789	9.02	0.45	135	0
A340	1	2	0.0	0.0	0.0	0	4	4	45.00	0.00	0	407
A330	13	14	0.0	10,762.6	10,762.6	539	34	573	50.00	1.70	512	3,600
C17	10	0	33,050.3	9,411.4	42,461.7	523	0	523	63.23	1.49	449	0
Total	210	28	55,800.0	37,200.0	93,000.0	3,636	67	3,703	0.00	5.89	1,772	5,717

Significant Results:

1. *Current Fleet closure of 73.59 well above 30 day goal*

2. *Capable of moving only 5.89 of required 10.17 MTM/D*

Table 25: Model CurR-2

Results	Closure =	30.17	Scenario 2: Rwanda w/Current Fleet (52.7k sTons Moved in 30 Days)									
Aircraft Type	# Acft Cargo	# Acft Pax	Outsize Tons	Bulk Tons	Total Tons	Cargo Missions	Pax Missions	Total Missions	Average Payload	MTM per Day	Tons per Day	Passengers per Day
AN124	4	0	9,214.1	5,241.8	14,455.8	87	0	87	107.11	1.02	306	0
A310	9	10	0.0	4,100.9	4,100.9	195	25	220	37.00	0.80	239	1,493
KC-10	3	0	0.0	714.1	714.1	39	0	39	32.60	0.14	42	0
KC767	1	2	0.0	0.0	0.0	0	4	4	33.00	0.00	0	217
C130H	107	0	0.0	1,416.6	1,416.6	658	0	658	3.77	0.28	82	0
C130J	62	0	0.0	2,303.1	2,303.1	448	0	448	9.02	0.45	134	0
A340	1	2	0.0	0.0	0.0	0	4	4	45.00	0.00	0	407
A330	13	14	0.0	8,708.4	8,708.4	305	34	339	50.00	1.70	510	3,600
C17	10	0	13,385.9	7,615.1	21,001.1	212	0	212	63.23	1.49	445	0
Total	210	28	22,600.0	30,100.0	52,700.0	1,944	67	2,011	0.00	5.89	1,758	5,717

Significant Results:

1. *Current Fleet can only move 56% of required cargo in 30 days*

Future Capacity

Table 26: Model FutR-1

Scenario 2: Rwanda w/Future Fleet (26.08 Days to Move All Requirements)											
Results	Closure =	26.08									
Aircraft Type	# Acft Cargo	# Acft Pax	Outsize Tons	Bulk Tons	Total Tons	Cargo Missions	Pax Missions	Total Missions	Average Payload	MTM per Day	Tons per Day	Passengers per Day
A310	7	10	0.0	1,766.9	1,766.9	120	21	141	37.00	0.57	171	1,466
KC-10	3	0	0.0	430.7	430.7	34	0	34	32.60	0.14	42	0
KC767	3	4	0.0	630.3	630.3	48	8	56	33.00	0.20	62	538
C130H	107	0	0.0	854.5	854.5	567	0	567	3.77	0.28	82	0
C130J	70	0	0.0	1,576.2	1,576.2	437	0	437	9.02	0.51	152	0
A340	2	4	0.0	429.8	429.8	24	8	32	45.00	0.14	43	1,009
A330	10	14	0.0	3,820.3	3,820.3	192	29	221	50.00	1.24	369	3,535
C17	10	0	9,256.1	4,593.4	13,849.6	182	0	182	63.23	1.49	444	0
A400M	170	0	46,543.9	23,097.8	69,641.6	2,722	0	2,722	21.22	7.49	2,221	0
Total	382	32	55,800.0	37,200.0	93,000.0	4,326	66	4,392	0.00	12.06	3,585	6,548

Significant Results:

1. *Future Fleet closure of 26.08 days within 30 day goal.*

Table 27: Model FutR-2

Scenario 2: Rwanda w/Future Fleet (93k sTons Moved in 30 Days)											
Results	Closure =	30.03									
Aircraft Type	# Acft Cargo	# Acft Pax	Outsize Tons	Bulk Tons	Total Tons	Cargo Missions	Pax Missions	Total Missions	Average Payload	MTM per Day	Tons per Day	Passengers per Day
A310	8	10	0.0	2,449.1	2,449.1	166	21	187	37.00	0.69	206	1,466
KC-10	3	0	0.0	497.5	497.5	39	0	39	32.60	0.14	42	0
KC767	3	4	0.0	728.1	728.1	56	8	64	33.00	0.20	61	538
C130H	107	0	0.0	987.1	987.1	655	0	655	3.77	0.28	82	0
C130J	70	0	0.0	1,820.7	1,820.7	505	0	505	9.02	0.51	152	0
A340	3	4	0.0	992.9	992.9	56	8	64	45.00	0.28	83	1,009
A330	11	14	0.0	4,964.4	4,964.4	249	29	278	50.00	1.39	416	3,535
C17	10	0	11,957.4	5,305.9	17,263.3	210	0	210	63.23	1.49	446	0
A400M	124	0	43,842.6	19,454.3	63,296.9	2,293	0	2,293	21.22	5.46	1,624	0
Total	339	32	55,800.0	37,200.0	93,000.0	4,229	66	4,295	0.00	10.44	3,112	6,548

Significant Results:

1. *Only 124 of projected 170 A400Ms required to complete full closure in 30 days.*

Alternate Capacity

A third set of model runs sought to determine how an expanded European fleet of C-17s would compare to the proposed addition of A400Ms. The researcher isolated A400M and C-17 allocated cargo from the time constrained model runs (FutB-2 & FutR-2). With the required A400Ms established from Models FutB-2 & Fut R-2, these models were then run substituting C-17s for A400Ms to determine the corresponding number of required C-17s to meet a 30 day force closure

Table 28: Model AltR-2

				Scenario 2: Rwanda w/Alternate Fleet (93k sTons Moved in 30 Days)								
Results	Closure =	30.30										
Aircraft	# Acft	# Acft	Outsize	Bulk	Total	Cargo	Pax	Total	Average	MTM	Tons	Passengers
Type	Cargo	Pax	Tons	Tons	Tons	Missions	Missions	Missions	Payload	per Day	per Day	per Day
A310	7	10	0.0	2,060.3	2,060.3	140	21	161	37.00	0.57	171	1,466
KC-10	3	0	0.0	502.3	502.3	39	0	39	32.60	0.14	42	0
KC767	3	4	0.0	735.0	735.0	56	8	64	33.00	0.20	62	538
C130H	107	0	0.0	996.4	996.4	661	0	661	3.77	0.28	82	0
C130J	70	0	0.0	1,838.0	1,838.0	510	0	510	9.02	0.51	152	0
A340	2	4	0.0	501.2	501.2	28	8	36	45.00	0.14	43	1,009
A330	10	14	0.0	4,454.8	4,454.8	223	29	252	50.00	1.24	371	3,535
C17	47	0	55,800.0	26,112.0	81,912.0	1,033	0	1,033	63.23	7.26	2,165	0
Total	249	32	55,800.0	37,200.0	93,000.0	2,690	66	2,756	0.00	10.34	3,088	6,548

Significant Results:

1. Only 47 C-17s required to complete closure in 30 days. (37 added to current fleet)

Algebraic Validation

Algebraic equations listed in AFPAM 10-1403 and further defined in *The Algebra of Airlift* article, were used to validate alternate fleet results determined by the AMPCALC model runs. These equations are actually the basis for the AMPCALC deterministic model, so when isolated without the additional refining variables of AMPCALC, gross solutions to the airlift gap questions are presented. Comparing the results between the simplified equations and the more comprehensive model show fairly similar results. The equations run to determine the fleet size required to obtain closure within 30 days. The deviation from AMPCALC's model results (in terms of aircraft required) can be seen at the bottom of the tables below. This method was only applied to the analysis of Scenarios 1 & 2.

Scenario 2: Rwanda		Scenario 2: Rwanda	
C-17		**A400M**	
Cargo Requirement	81912.02	Cargo Requirement	63296.90
Average Payload	63.23	Average Payload	21.22
Number of Cargo Msns	1295.46	Number of Cargo Msns	2982.89
Leg1 Flying Distance	3297.00	Leg1 Flying Distance	3297.00
Leg1 Block Speed	407.00	Leg1 Block Speed	338.00
Leg1 Flying Time	8.10	Leg1 Flying Time	9.75
Leg2 Flying Distance	0.00	Leg2 Flying Distance	0.00
Leg2 Block Speed	1.00	Leg2 Block Speed	1.00
Leg2 Flying Time	0.00	Leg2 Flying Time	0.00
Total 1 Way Fly Time	8.10	Total 1 Way Fly Time	9.75
Return Flying Distance	3297.00	Return Flying Distance	3297.00
Return Block Speed	407.00	Return Block Speed	338.00
Return Flying Time	8.10	Return Flying Time	9.75
Round Trip Flying Time	16.20	Round Trip Flying Time	19.51
Round Trip Distance	6594.00	Round Trip Distance	6594.00
Avg Block Speed	407.00	Avg Block Speed	338.00
Onload Time	4.00	Onload Time	4.00
Enroute Stop Time	2.50	Enroute Stop Time	2.50
Num of Enroute Stops	0.00	Num of Enroute Stops	0.00
Offload Times	3.25	Offload Times	2.75
Total Gnd Time	7.25	Total Gnd Time	6.75
Cycle Time	23.45	Cycle Time	26.26
Station Ground Time	2.75	Station Ground Time	2.75
Station Capability	999.00	Station Capability	999.00
Station Interval	0.00	Station Interval	0.00
Total Aircraft Inventory	54.00	Total Aircraft Inventory	140.00
Backup Aircraft Inventory	0.00	Backup Aircraft Inventory	0.00
Training Fence (5%)	2.70	Training Fence (5%)	7.00
Primary Msn Acft Inventory	51.30	Primary Msn Acft Inventory	133.00
Aircraft Allocation Interval	0.46	Aircraft Allocation Interval	0.20
MC Rate	0.85	MC Rate	0.85
Scenario Use Rate	16.58	Scenario Use Rate	17.83
Objective Ute Rate	13.43	Objective Ute Rate	14.43
Flying Hour Capability Interval	0.56	Flying Hour Capability Interval	0.24
Flow Interval	0.56	Flow Interval	0.24
Closure	30.78	Closure	30.72
Prime Aircraft Required	41.56	Prime Aircraft Required	107.62
Tons per Day	2689.07	Tons per Day	2087.25
Ute Rate	13.43	Ute Rate	14.43
Actual Productivity Factor	0.50	Actual Productivity Factor	0.50
MTM/D	8.87	MTM/D	6.88
% Deviation from AMCALC	0.08	% Deviation from AMCALC	0.07
(Acft req'd for 30 day closure)		(Acft req'd for 30 day closure)	

Significant Results:

　　　1. 51 C-17 required vs. 47 calculated by AMCALC (8.38% Difference)

　　　2. 133 A400M required vs. 124 calculated by AMCALC (6.77% Difference)

Scenario 2 Analysis

Scenario 2, transporting a large NRF to Rwanda included the largest required cargo loads. As with scenario 1, MTM/D algebra and modeling concluded that a significant gap exists in Europe's current airlift fleet, yet their future fleet should have adequate capacity, baring barriers to MRTT aircraft providing cargo support.

Europe's current fleet of aircraft were able to produce full force closure in 73.59 days, significantly missing the 30 day goal. The 5.89 MTM/D capability fell far short of the calculated 10.17 MTM/D requirement. Running the model with a 30 day limit on transport, the current fleet was only capable of moving 56% of the required 93k s/Tons nearly mirroring MTM/D calculated shortfalls. Once again, passenger movement were not a factor, however the shortage of cargo lift may be even more significant when one considers the lack of infrastructure in Africa. This model assumed MRTT aircraft would be useful in transporting both passengers and cargo. By moving cargo off MRTT aircraft for this scenario, force closure jumps to nearly 92 days. In reality, poor infrastructure and lack of adequate airfields may significantly increase the airlift gap for certain operations.

Using the full fleet of 170 A400Ms, the model results showed force closure in 26.08 days. Restricting the model to 30 days, shows a minimum of 124 A400Ms are required for force closure. Again these results included MRTT aircraft in a cargo role. With MRTT aircraft restricted to passenger transport to nearby airfields, force closure for the full 170 A400M fleet grows from 26.08 days to 32.05 days. When the model is run to minimize the number of A400M required to meet the 30 day goal, the result is 185.

If MRTT aircraft are further prohibited from passenger transport, the number of required A400Ms only slightly increases. With zero MRTT support, AMCALC shows passenger closure can be completed by using less than 40 C-130H aircraft for passenger transport. For the Rwanda scenario C-130H were limited to an average payload of only 3.77 s/Tons/Day, therefore only 3 additional A400M aircraft were required to make up the difference in the cargo capacity lost by using a portion of the C-130 fleet for passenger movement. With MRTT lift available, the future fleet does appear to fill the current gap. Without MRTT support however the additional 170 A400Ms projected to Europe's fleet falls just short of meeting contingency timetables.

Analysis of C-17s replacing A400Ms concludes 47 are required to meet a 30 day force closure. This result indicates the purchase of an additional 37 C-17 aircraft may replace the purchase of 170 A400M aircraft for this central African scenario. When run again without the use of MRTT airlift, the number of required C-17s is 60. Under these constraints adding 50 C-17s to the British and SAC fleets could substitute for the 185 required A400M. Many significant assumptions and second order effects of such an alternate fleet due exist however, and are further described in the discussion section of this paper.

Scenario 3: Mali

Table 30: Scenario 3 Requirements

Scenario Requirements				
Scenario	Cargo (s/Tons)	Distance (NM)	Deploy (Days)	MTM/D
3. Mali (consisted of 6 Battalions transported from 4 locations)				
3a. Eur Battalion x3	22,577	2,025	10	4.572
3b. Afr Battalion x1	2,004	1,015	10	0.203
3c. Afr Battalion x1	2,004	856	10	0.172
3d. Afr Battalion x1	2,004	541	10	0.108

For the Mali scenario, varying sized forces were airlifted from four separate locations. Therefore, each of the Mali scenario routes consists of a separate results table for each of the battalions transported.

To optimize the use of each fleet input to AMCALC the program's integration feature was used. The Integrate Cycles application allows the researcher to spread the available aircraft across any/all cycle combinations according to the percentage of the total cargo and passenger requirements (AMPCALC User's Manual, 2010).

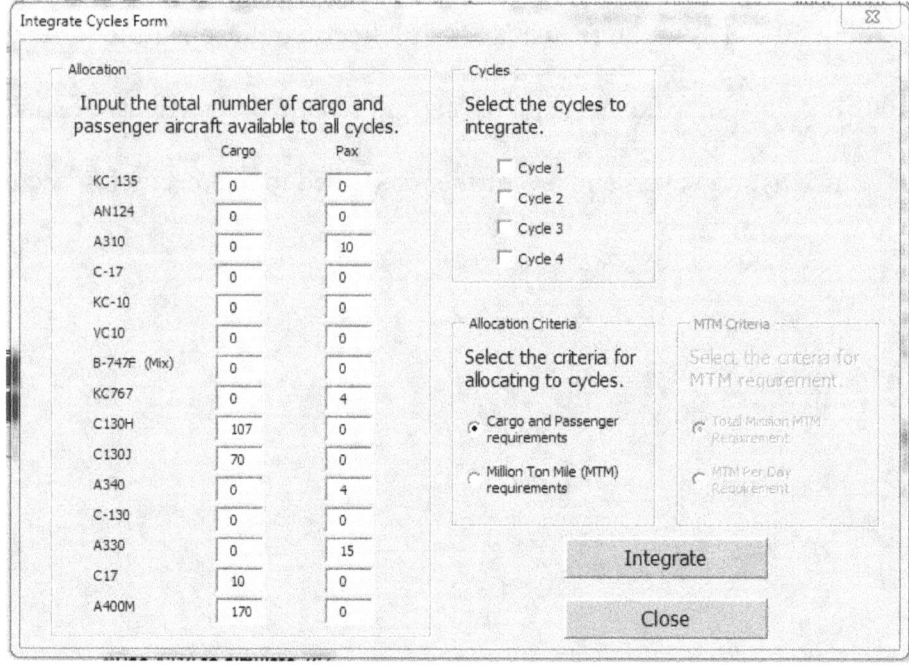

Figure 19: AMPCALC Cycle Integration Screen Shot

94

Current Capacity

Table 31: Model CurM-1a

Results	Closure =	16.53	Scenario 3: Mali w/Current Fleet (16.53 Days to Move 3 EU Battalions)									
Aircraft	# Acft	# Acft	Outsize	Bulk	Total	Cargo	Pax	Total	Average	MTM	Tons	Passengers
Type	Cargo	Pax	Tons	Tons	Tons	Missions	Missions	Missions	Payload	per Day	per Day	per Day
C130H	84	0	0.0	3,337.5	3,337.5	462	0	462	13.31	0.77	372	0
C130J	49	0	0.0	3,094.1	3,094.1	301	0	301	18.94	0.72	346	0
A330	0	3	0.0	0.0	0.0	0	14	14	50.00	0.00	0	1,079
C17	8	0	10,314.0	5,831.4	16,145.4	135	0	135	80.00	1.35	654	0
Total	141	3	10,314.0	12,263.0	22,577.0	898	14	912	0.00	2.84	1,371	1,079

Table 32: Model CurM-1b

Results	Closure =	14.32	Scenario 3: Mali w/Current Fleet (14.32 Days to Move 1st African Battalion)									
Aircraft	# Acft	# Acft	Outsize	Bulk	Total	Cargo	Pax	Total	Average	MTM	Tons	Passengers
Type	Cargo	Pax	Tons	Tons	Tons	Missions	Missions	Missions	Payload	per Day	per Day	per Day
C130H	8	0	0.0	1,092.1	1,092.1	67	0	67	17.50	0.08	82	0
C130J	4	0	0.0	775.9	775.9	37	0	37	22.50	0.06	59	0
A330	0	2	0.0	0.0	0.0	0	3	3	50.00	0.00	0	871
C17	1	0	0.0	0.0	0.0	0	0	0	80.00	0.00	0	0
Total	13	2	0.0	1,868.0	1,868.0	104	3	107	0.00	0.14	141	871

Table 33: Model CurM-1c

Results	Closure =	13.08	Scenario 3: Mali w/Current Fleet (13.08 Days to Move 2nd African Battalion)									
Aircraft	# Acft	# Acft	Outsize	Bulk	Total	Cargo	Pax	Total	Average	MTM	Tons	Passengers
Type	Cargo	Pax	Tons	Tons	Tons	Missions	Missions	Missions	Payload	per Day	per Day	per Day
C130H	8	0	0.0	1,061.5	1,061.5	66	0	66	17.50	0.08	87	0
C130J	4	0	0.0	806.5	806.5	39	0	39	22.50	0.06	67	0
A330	0	2	0.0	0.0	0.0	0	3	3	50.00	0.00	0	924
C17	1	0	0.0	0.0	0.0	0	0	0	80.00	0.00	0	0
Total	13	2	0.0	1,868.0	1,868.0	105	3	108	0.00	0.13	154	924

Table 34: Model CurM-1d

Results	Closure =	7.86	Scenario 3: Mali w/Current Fleet (7.86 Days to Move 3rd African Battalion)									
Aircraft	# Acft	# Acft	Outsize	Bulk	Total	Cargo	Pax	Total	Average	MTM	Tons	Passengers
Type	Cargo	Pax	Tons	Tons	Tons	Missions	Missions	Missions	Payload	per Day	per Day	per Day
C130H	7	0	0.0	843.1	843.1	52	0	52	17.50	0.06	115.01	0
C130J	5	0	0.0	1,024.9	1,024.9	49	0	49	22.50	0.08	140.68	0
Total	12	2	0.0	1,868.0	1,868.0	101	3	104	0	0.14	255.69	1087

Significant Results:

1. Current Fleet closure of 16.53 well above 10 day goal

2. Capable of moving only 3.25 of required 5.05 MTM/D

Table 35: Model CurM-2a

Scenario 3: Mali w/Current Fleet (15.05k of 22.6k sTons Moved in ~10 Days [3 EU Battalions])											
Results	Closure =	11.21									
Aircraft	# Acft	# Acft	Outsize	Bulk	Total	Cargo	Pax	Total	Average	MTM	Tons	Passengers
Type	Cargo	Pax	Tons	Tons	Tons	Missions	Missions	Missions	Payload	per Day	per Day	per Day
C130H	83	0	0.0	2,202.0	2,202.0	305	0	305	13.31	0.76	361	0
C130J	49	0	0.0	2,070.6	2,070.6	202	0	202	18.94	0.72	341	0
A330	0	3	0.0	0.0	0.0	0	14	14	50.00	0.00	0	1,079
C17	8	0	6,875.0	3,902.4	10,777.4	90	0	90	80.00	1.35	651	0
Total	140	3	6,875.0	8,175.0	15,050.0	597	14	611	0.00	2.83	1,353	1,079

Table 36: Model CurM-2b

Scenario 3: Mali w/Current Fleet (1.8k of 2.0k sTons Moved in ~10 Days [1st African Battalion])											
Results	Closure =	10.82									
Aircraft	# Acft	# Acft	Outsize	Bulk	Total	Cargo	Pax	Total	Average	MTM	Tons	Passengers
Type	Cargo	Pax	Tons	Tons	Tons	Missions	Missions	Missions	Payload	per Day	per Day	per Day
C130H	10	0	0.0	1,092.1	1,092.1	67	0	67	17.50	0.11	108	0
C130J	5	0	0.0	775.9	775.9	37	0	37	22.50	0.08	78	0
A330	0	1	0.0	0.0	0.0	0	3	3	50.00	0.00	0	871
C17	1	0	0.0	0.0	0.0	0	0	0	80.00	0.00	0	0
Total	16	2	0.0	1,868.0	1,868.0	104	3	107	0.00	0.19	186	871

Table 37: Model CurM-2c

Scenario 3: Mali w/Current Fleet (1.8k of 2.0k sTons Moved in ~10 Days [2nd African Battalion])											
Results	Closure =	10.92									
Aircraft	# Acft	# Acft	Outsize	Bulk	Total	Cargo	Pax	Total	Average	MTM	Tons	Passengers
Type	Cargo	Pax	Tons	Tons	Tons	Missions	Missions	Missions	Payload	per Day	per Day	per Day
C130H	7	0	0.0	741.4	741.4	46	0	46	17.50	0.06	73	0
C130J	6	0	0.0	1,126.6	1,126.6	54	0	54	22.50	0.10	111	0
A330	0	1	0.0	0.0	0.0	0	3	3	50.00	0.00	0	924
C17	1	0	0.0	0.0	0.0	0	0	0	80.00	0.00	0	0
Total	14	2	0.0	1,868.0	1,868.0	100	3	103	0.00	0.16	184	924

Table 38: Model CurM-2d

Scenario 3: Mali w/Current Fleet (1.8k of 2.0k sTons Moved in ~10 Days [3rd African Battalion])											
Results	Closure =	10.85									
Aircraft	# Acft	# Acft	Outsize	Bulk	Total	Cargo	Pax	Total	Average	MTM	Tons	Passengers
Type	Cargo	Pax	Tons	Tons	Tons	Missions	Missions	Missions	Payload	per Day	per Day	per Day
C130H	6	0	0.0	1,161.8	1,161.8	72	0	72	17.50	0.06	114.91	0
C130J	3	0	0.0	706.2	706.2	34	0	34	22.50	0.04	71.10	0
A330	0	1	0.0	0.0	0.0	0	3	3	50.00	0.00	0	1,087
Total	9	2	0.0	1,868.0	1,868.0	106	3	109	0	0.10	186.02	1087

Significant Results:

1. Current Fleet can only move 71% of required cargo in 10 days

Future Capacity

Table 39: Model FutM-1a

	Scenario 3: Mali w/Future Fleet (3.78 Days to Move 3 EU Battalions)											
Results	Closure =	3.78										
Aircraft	# Acft	# Acft	Outsize	Bulk	Total	Cargo	Pax	Total	Average	MTM	Tons	Passengers
Type	Cargo	Pax	Tons	Tons	Tons	Missions	Missions	Missions	Payload	per Day	per Day	per Day
A310	0	7	0.0	0.0	0.0	0	6	6	37.00	0.00	0	1,199
KC767	0	3	0.0	0.0	0.0	0	3	3	33.00	0.00	0	545
C130H	84	0	0.0	691.1	691.1	96	0	96	13.31	0.77	336	0
C130J	55	0	0.0	718.9	718.9	70	0	70	18.94	0.81	355	0
A340	0	3	0.0	0.0	0.0	0	3	3	45.00	0.00	0	1,022
A330	0	9	0.0	0.0	0.0	0	8	8	50.00	0.00	0	2,834
C17	8	0	1,147.6	1,207.5	2,355.1	28	0	28	80.00	1.35	616	0
A400M	134	0	9,166.4	9,645.5	18,811.9	457	0	457	38.90	10.80	4,747	0
Total	281	22	10,314.0	12,263.0	22,577.0	651	20	671	0.00	13.73	6,054	5,600

Table 40: Model FutM-1b

	Scenario 3: Mali w/Future Fleet (2.46 Days to Move 1st African Battalion)											
Results	Closure =	2.46										
Aircraft	# Acft	# Acft	Outsize	Bulk	Total	Cargo	Pax	Total	Average	MTM	Tons	Passengers
Type	Cargo	Pax	Tons	Tons	Tons	Missions	Missions	Missions	Payload	per Day	per Day	per Day
C130H	8	0	0.0	169.7	169.7	11	0	11	17.50	0.08	74	0
C130J	5	0	0.0	160.7	160.7	8	0	8	22.50	0.08	74	0
A340	0	0	0.0	0.0	0.0	0	0	0	45.00	0.00	0	0
A330	0	2	0.0	0.0	0.0	0	3	3	50.00	0.00	0	871
A400M	12	0	136.0	1,537.6	1,673.6	41	0	41	40.50	0.76	670	0
Total	26	3	136.0	1,868.0	2,004.0	60	3	63	0.00	0.92	818	871

Table 41: Model FutM-1c

	Scenario 3: Mali w/Future Fleet (2.41 Days to Move 2nd African Battalion)											
Results	Closure =	2.41										
Aircraft	# Acft	# Acft	Outsize	Bulk	Total	Cargo	Pax	Total	Average	MTM	Tons	Passengers
Type	Cargo	Pax	Tons	Tons	Tons	Missions	Missions	Missions	Payload	per Day	per Day	per Day
C130H	8	0	0.0	176.1	176.1	11	0	11	17.50	0.08	83	0
C130J	5	0	0.0	178.4	178.4	9	0	9	22.50	0.08	84	0
A330	0	2	0.0	0.0	0.0	0	3	3	50.00	0.00	0	924
A400M	12	0	136.0	1,513.6	1,649.6	41	0	41	40.50	0.66	675	0
Total	26	3	136.0	1,868.0	2,004.0	61	3	64	0.00	0.81	842	924

Table 42: Model FutM-1d

	Scenario 3: Mali w/Future Fleet (1.91 Days to Move 3rd African Battalion)											
Results	Closure =	1.91										
Aircraft	# Acft	# Acft	Outsize	Bulk	Total	Cargo	Pax	Total	Average	MTM	Tons	Passengers
Type	Cargo	Pax	Tons	Tons	Tons	Missions	Missions	Missions	Payload	per Day	per Day	per Day
C130H	7	0	0.0	185.0	185.0	12	0	12	17.50	0.06	104	0
C130J	5	0	0.0	224.9	224.9	11	0	11	22.50	0.08	132	0
A330	0	2	0.0	0.0	0.0	0	3	3	50.00	0.00	0	1,087
A400M	12	0	136.0	1,458.1	1,594.1	39	0	39	40.50	0.50	819	0
Total	24	5	136.0	1,868.0	2,004.0	62	3	65	0.00	0.64	1,056	1,087

Significant Results:

1. Future Fleet closure of 3.78 days well within 30 day goal

To move requirements within 10 days, all aircraft were integrated to optimize their

97

allocation with the exception of the A400M. Modeling the African battalion movements separately, the researcher determined that only one 1 additional aircraft is required to fulfill all outsize cargo needs for the all 3 African battalions within 10 days. Similar results were found when examining the alternate fleet of C-17s in place of A400Ms. Results can be seen in Tables 43 - 47.

Table 43: Model FutM-2a

Scenario 3: Mali w/Future Fleet (22.6k sTons Moved in ~10 Days [3 EU Battalions])												
Results	Closure =	9.93										
Aircraft	# Acft	# Acft	Outsize	Bulk	Total	Cargo	Pax	Total	Average	MTM	Tons	Passengers
Type	Cargo	Pax	Tons	Tons	Tons	Missions	Missions	Missions	Payload	per Day	per Day	per Day
A310	0	7	0.0	0.0	0.0	0	6	6	37.00	0.00	0	1,199
KC767	0	3	0.0	0.0	0.0	0	3	3	33.00	0.00	0	545
C130H	81	0	0.0	1,882.8	1,882.8	261	0	261	13.31	0.74	349	0
C130J	56	0	0.0	2,089.2	2,089.2	204	0	204	18.94	0.82	388	0
A340	0	3	0.0	0.0	0.0	0	3	3	45.00	0.00	0	1,022
A330	0	9	0.0	0.0	0.0	0	8	8	50.00	0.00	0	2,834
C17	8	0	4,273.0	3,434.9	7,707.8	80	0	80	80.00	1.35	643	0
A400M	24	0	6,041.0	4,856.1	10,897.1	230	0	230	38.90	1.91	908	0
Total	169	22	10,314.0	12,263.0	22,577.0	775	20	795	0.00	4.83	2,288	5,600

Table 44: Model FutM-2b

Scenario 3: Mali w/Future Fleet (1.8k sTons Moved in ~10 Days [1st African Battalion])												
Results	Closure =	10.22										
Aircraft	# Acft	# Acft	Outsize	Bulk	Total	Cargo	Pax	Total	Average	MTM	Tons	Passengers
Type	Cargo	Pax	Tons	Tons	Tons	Missions	Missions	Missions	Payload	per Day	per Day	per Day
C130H	11	0	0.0	1,144.9	1,144.9	71	0	71	17.50	0.13	120	0
C130J	5	0	0.0	723.1	723.1	35	0	35	22.50	0.08	77	0
A330	0	1	0.0	0.0	0.0	0	3	3	50.00	0.00	0	871
Total	18	3	0.0	1,868.0	1,868.0	106	3	109	0.00	0.21	197	871

Table 45: Model FutM-2c

Scenario 3: Mali w/Future Fleet (1.8k sTons Moved in ~10 Days [2nd African Battalion])												
Results	Closure =	9.89										
Aircraft	# Acft	# Acft	Outsize	Bulk	Total	Cargo	Pax	Total	Average	MTM	Tons	Passengers
Type	Cargo	Pax	Tons	Tons	Tons	Missions	Missions	Missions	Payload	per Day	per Day	per Day
C130H	10	0	0.0	1,061.5	1,061.5	66	0	66	17.50	0.10	115	0
C130J	5	0	0.0	806.5	806.5	39	0	39	22.50	0.08	89	0
A330	0	1	0.0	0.0	0.0	0	3	3	50.00	0.00	0	924
Total	17	3	0.0	1,868.0	1,868.0	105	3	108	0.00	0.18	204	924

Table 46: Model FutM-2d

Scenario 3: Mali w/Future Fleet (1.8k sTons Moved in ~10 Days [3rd African Battalion])												
Results	Closure =	10.14										
Aircraft	# Acft	# Acft	Outsize	Bulk	Total	Cargo	Pax	Total	Average	MTM	Tons	Passengers
Type	Cargo	Pax	Tons	Tons	Tons	Missions	Missions	Missions	Payload	per Day	per Day	per Day
C130H	5	0	0.0	873.1	873.1	54	0	54	17.50	0.05	92	0
C130J	4	0	0.0	994.9	994.9	48	0	48	22.50	0.06	105	0
A330	0	1	0.0	0.0	0.0	0	3	3	50.00	0.00	0	1,087
Total	10	5	0.0	1,868.0	1,868.0	102	3	105	0.00	0.11	198	1,087

Significant Results:

1. Only 25 of projected 170 A400Ms required to complete full closure in 10 days

Alternate Capacity

	Scenario 3: Mali w/Alternate Fleet (10.61 Days to Move 3 EU Battalions)											
Results	Closure =	10.61										
Aircraft	# Acft	# Acft	Outsize	Bulk	Total	Cargo	Pax	Total	Average	MTM	Tons	Passengers
Type	Cargo	Pax	Tons	Tons	Tons	Missions	Missions	Missions	Payload	per Day	per Day	per Day
A310	0	7	0.0	0.0	0.0	0	6	6	37.00	0.00	0	1,199
KC767	0	3	0.0	0.0	0.0	0	3	3	33.00	0.00	0	545
C130H	84	0	0.0	2,104.9	2,104.9	292	0	292	13.31	0.77	365	0
C130J	55	0	0.0	2,189.4	2,189.4	213	0	213	18.94	0.81	382	0
A340	0	3	0.0	0.0	0.0	0	3	3	45.00	0.00	0	1,022
A330	0	10	0.0	0.0	0.0	0	9	9	50.00	0.00	0	3,188
C17	16	0	10,314.0	7,968.6	18,282.6	184	0	184	80.00	2.93	1,398	0
Total	155	23	10,314.0	12,263.0	22,577.0	689	21	710	0.00	4.51	2,146	5,955

Significant Results:

> *1. Only 17 C-17s required to complete full closure in 10 days (7 added to current fleet)*

Scenario 3 Analysis

Scenario 3, transporting a rapid response force similar to that used for Mali's real-world operation in 2013, aimed for a 10 day timeline. As with scenario 1, MTM/D algebra and modeling concluded that a significant gap exists in Europe's current airlift fleet, yet their future fleet should have adequate capacity to meet stated goals.

Referencing real-world events and the EADS 2012 study, this scenario was limited to C-130, C-17 and A400M aircraft for cargo transport. The current fleet of available aircraft was able to close airlift from Europe and all three African locations in 16.53 days. The ability to only lift 3.25 of the required 5.05 MTM/D was significant. If only given 10 days for airlift, the current fleet would fall 29% short of transporting all requirements according to AMCALC.

Using the future fleet of A400Ms and additional C-130Js however, force closure results are achieved in less than 4 days. Two of the African battalions may actually be moved in less than 2 days. Running AMCALC to minimize the A400M fleet shows only

25 are necessary to close within 10 days. This greatly reduced number is significant when one considers that the researcher still used MRTT aircraft to transport passengers in this scenario. It is highly feasible that this transport may not be available in a scenario such as this, requiring austere airfield capable aircraft such as the C-130, A400M and C-17 to carry both cargo and passengers. When the model is run without the use of any MRTT aircraft, results show that a small increase in A400M numbers in coordination with C-130 passenger transport adequately meet all requirements within stated timetables. Using 27 C-130 for passenger transport and bringing the total A400M fleet up to 28, all passenger and cargo requirements are met within 10 days.

Similarly low numbers result from modeling the alternate fleet of C-17s. Only 16 total C-17s are required to meet all requirements within 10 days. Again the need to purchase only 6 additional aircraft, shows that for this scenario, only a modest addition to the current fleet is necessary to meet objectives.

Hypothesis Results

In framing the research questions, 3 hypothesis were submitted.

H1: The strategic airlift capability provided by Europe's current airlift fleet and resource pooling agreements of NATO and EU countries fall short of meeting stated contingency goals.

The data clearly supports H1. The basic MTM/D math, algebra based spreadsheets, and AMPCALC models all show significant shortfalls in the European fleet. The most adverse scenario shows a shortfall of 8 C-130J and 188 A400M aircraft, while the least dramatic still indicated a 25 aircraft shortfall.

H2: Fulfillment of the scheduled A400M procurement will adequately addresses NATO strategic airlift shortfalls.

The data from this research supports H2, although not conclusively. Scenario 2 to Rwanda, indicated that an additional 15 A400M would be required above and beyond the 170 on order. This shortfall only pertains to operations with large, heavy NRF movements where MRTT aircraft are not available for cargo use. When MRTT aircraft operations are prohibited the number increases to 18 additional A400M. All other scenario results do show the projected European fleet to be adequate in meeting all objectives.

H3: Expansion of European owned C-17s will adequately addresses NATO strategic airlift shortfalls.

The data supports H3. In each scenario, the addition of relatively few C-17s addressed strategic airlift shortfalls. The number of additional aircraft is only relative when compared to the equivalent number of A400Ms that would be required to obtain the same results. The number of additional aircraft is quite significant when considering one model in particular required NATO to increase its C-17 fleet by 500% to reach objectives. The feasibility of this alternate fleet, the total cost of each aircraft and others factors is further described in the discussion section of this paper.

V. Discussion

This research attempted to identify any existing European shortfall of strategic airlift and to quantify its current and future size. Although many of the research assumptions and limitations were identified within the methodology section of this paper, other significant aspects of the research are open for criticism and further discussion.

Scenario Weaknesses

Having research based heavily on models and their results opens multiple avenues of criticism. Even with a perfect representation of the aircraft performance, which is of course unobtainable, how the fleet is employed by the researcher will significantly steer results. Although the researcher worked to build realistic and feasible scenarios, many assumptions were made to both simplify the model and focus research on only the strategic airlift aspects of deployment.

Of the glaring weaknesses of the scenarios is the unlikely absence of any U.S. or Canadian airlift support. Any operation meaningful enough to garner the support and involvement of all European NATO and PfP nations would undoubtedly include some form of North American involvement as well. Scenario 1 to the Bahamas, is the most unlikely to forego non-European allies considering its geographic location and political ties. The absence of these allies in the research although necessary to focus on European strategic airlift, surely skewed results. The resulting aircraft fleet predictions would likely be much smaller as U.S. and Canadian capabilities would help to augment any future European airlift fleet to meet operational goals.

Many other assumptions within the scenarios would likely increase fleet requirements if removed. Aircraft capacity and capability for example was input in a very optimistic

102

manner. Aircraft frequently cube out due to volume constraints well before meeting weight limitations. This is particularly true with over and outsized cargo, which this research found to be significant. This research used only weight to define aircraft capacity. In only using weight a reduction of aircraft capability could have been included to more realistically simulate predicted cargo loads. AFPAM 10-1403 actually applies this very concept for planners by differentiating between actual and planning payloads (AFPAM 10-1403, 2011). Table 3 of AFPAM 10-1403 limits planning payloads to 69% for the C-17 and as little as 53% for aircraft such as the KC-10. The researcher acknowledges that meeting maximum weight limitations on each sortie is not feasible, yet estimating weight penalties below aircraft capabilities across thousands of sorties would inject a sizeable level of obscurity to the research. Instead the researcher chose to model the optimum payload capabilities, acknowledging the inaccuracy of this assumption.

Further limiting the ability to transport max weight loads on sorties would be the availability of cargo for each aircraft. It is unlikely that payload would be prepositioned and properly configured for loading as each aircraft arrived for upload at each APOE. Partial loads and/or delays to departures would surely occur when accounting for thousands of cargo tons transported on thousands of sorties. The availability of cargo further detracts from scenario realism when one considers the resulting force closure times. Significant intratheater transport would be required to consolidate cargo for large airlift payloads. This research does not account for the time required to prepare and move cargo to APOE, but only the time required to deliver cargo from APOEs to APODs.

The use of sealift was briefly discussed earlier in this paper, but does deserve another mention. Multimodal transport is a proven logistics strategy. Given the austere financial condition of the participants' defense budgets, the cost effectiveness of sealift may trump the speed of airlift. This point is further emphasized when one considers that velocity may actually increase with sealift for large, heavy loads carried over great distances. Again this aspect of likely transport was not included in the research to simplify the model and focus on airlift only.

Alternate Fleet

Given the ease at which AMCALC could manipulate fleets configurations, the researcher explored the use of C-17s in place of A400Ms. There had been discussion of procuring such a fleet, and many aspects of this research indicated that it may be advantageous. There are of course many political forces at play when purchasing large numbers of high value assets like these. It should not be surprising that European nations have chosen to procure European built aircraft. Looking beyond the political and national aspects of this decision however, there is quantitative data to support both the A400M purchase or the purchase of additional C-17s.

Capability

As an alternate to A400M, results from scenarios 1 & 2 indicate that a much smaller number of C-17s.

Table 48: A400M/C-17 Required per Scenario

A400M vs C-17		
Scenario	A400M Req'd	C-17 Req'd (added to current)
Bahamas	89	28
Rwanda	124	37
Mali	25	7

The smaller fleet required to meet scenario objectives would have the advantages of less crew required and less impact on MOG. Crew requirements in particular are significant considering comparable crew sizes for each aircraft type. MOG constitutes a slightly less than a one for one ratio of effect due to the C-17's greater size and capacity per aircraft. Within the scope of these scenarios with a limited number of APOEs and APODs the smaller fleet of C-17s would have many logistical advantages.

The larger fleet of A400M aircraft has benefits of its own however. The C -17 can carry up to 134 passengers, where the A400M is capable of 116. Having similar capability in this regard serves as a distinct advantage for the larger fleet of A400M. Deployment of large passenger movements would benefit from the flexibility afforded by the numerous A400Ms allocated to the operation. Even with partial loads optimized for mixed cargo and passenger movements, the A400Ms carrying capacity would benefit planners with a greater number of seats available across the fleet.

Similar to the advantage of passenger movement, the larger fleet of A400Ms would provide substantially more cubic volume in two of the three scenarios modeled. Using cargo bay capacities in Figure 17, the advantages of more A400M for a given cargo weight requirement can be seen in Table 49.

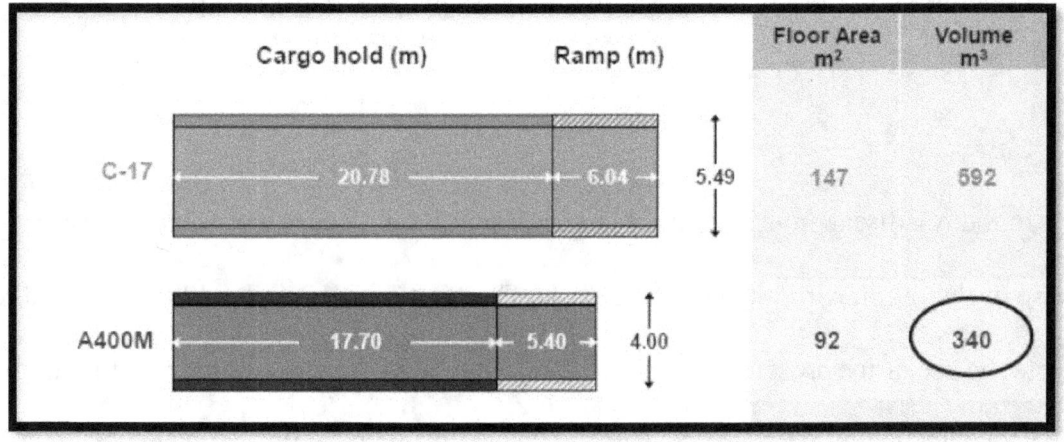

Figure 20: A400M/C-17 Cargo Hold

Table 49: A400M/C-17 Area & Volume per Scenario

Area and Volume Capacity			
Area m2	Bahamas	Rwanda	Mali
C-17	5,586	6,909	2,499
A400M	8,188	11,408	2,300
Volume m3	Bahamas	Rwanda	Mali
C-17	22,496	27,824	10,064
A400M	30,260	42,160	8,500

Where determining the number of aircraft required by weight may render the two fleets equal, the corresponding cargo area and volume is not. This may be a particular advantage for the transport of medium or low density payloads.

The A400M may have two more advantages not clearly depicted in this research. EADS refers to the A400M capability as "combat delivery to the point of need" (EADS brochure, 2012). The ability to use short unprepared airfields is touted as the A400M's differentiating advantage over other strategic airlift platforms. While the C-17 is also capable of using short, unprepared airfields, EADS pre-operational data does suggest the A400M has an advantage. Secondly, the A400M can be air to air refueling capable as both a tanker and receiver. This dual air to air role is a capability not explored within the bounds of this research, but is perhaps a significant attribute swaying European purchases.

Cost

In today's fiscal environment, it is inappropriate to discuss any weapon system purchase or operation without evaluating cost. The fleet of C-17 and A400M required to complete the scenarios presented in this research may lead the casual observer to question why the European do not simply buy less C-17 aircraft to obtain the same capability. Cost my further support this course of action. From a procurement standpoint alone, the cost to supplement the current European airlift fleet for each of the given scenario can be seen in Table 50. The cost per aircraft for any weapon system can be extremely difficult to determine. Costs vary from customer to customer, by time in a production line's life cycle, and by the number of units purchased. Table 50 also presents high, medium, low and average cost estimates for C-17 and A400M according to industry press releases and multiple associated press findings.

Table 50: A400M/C-17 Cost per Scenario

Cost for Required Aircraft			
C17	Bahamas	Rwanda	Mali
Est Cost	28	37	7
$300M	$8,400,000,000	$11,100,000,000	$2,100,000,000
$250M	$7,000,000,000	$9,250,000,000	$1,750,000,000
$202M	$5,656,000,000	$7,474,000,000	$1,414,000,000
$Avg	$7,019,000,000	$9,275,000,000	$1,755,000,000
A400M	Bahamas	Rwanda	Mali
Est Cost	89	124	25
$170M	$15,130,000,000	$21,080,000,000	$4,250,000,000
$125M	$11,125,000,000	$15,500,000,000	$3,125,000,000
$80M	$7,120,000,000	$9,920,000,000	$2,000,000,000
$Avg	$11,125,000,000	$15,500,000,000	$3,125,000,000
C-17 Cost Advantage			
High $	$6,730,000,000	$9,980,000,000	$2,150,000,000
Med $	$4,125,000,000	$6,250,000,000	$1,375,000,000
Low $	$1,464,000,000	$2,446,000,000	$586,000,000
Avg $	$4,106,333,333	$6,225,333,333	$1,370,333,333
Savings (using avg cost)	$4,106,000,000	$6,225,000,000	$1,370,000,000

Procurement costs do not tell the whole story however. The cost for each of the fleets described above must be considered in terms of total life cycle cost. The larger fleet of aircraft would require more maintenance and logistics men and equipment, more air crew and more training for the personnel. Each of these logistical areas would also be new for the A400M vs. the established supply chain for the C-17. Adding additional C-17s would eliminate a layer of complexity and cost to the fleet's logistics by reducing the number of aircraft variants (maintain the status-quo), and standardizing fleets with North American allies.

From an operational perspective, the larger fleets would require more crew, ramp space and fuel as well. Although promoted as more fuel efficient than the C-17, the efficiency would need to be quite substantial. For each of the three scenarios presented, the A400M fleet required 134%, 163% and 47% more aircraft respectively. Equivalent levels of fuel savings per aircraft would be required before any fuel savings were realized.

Conclusion

Europe's current strategic airlift shortfall is significant. Given capabilities, initiatives and priorities stated by NATO and the EU, a substantial gap exists between what is available and what is desired. This research supports the projected 2020 fleet of European aircraft to meet strategic airlift goals. The fulfillment of A400M orders will not only help Europeans become a global contingency partner of NATO, but will allow these allies to act and operate on their own for strictly European operations. Deployment of the NRF will likely be done using multimodal transportation, but the future fleet of European aircraft should enable the rapid deployment of even the largest NRF forces.

Recommendations

Examination of European defense initiatives would benefit from further research into the transport of forces. More clearly defined scenarios which include all modes of transport to include sealift would be beneficial. While exercises of smaller scale establish perhaps the best look at how forces deploy, simulating large scale deployments at significant distance provide a look at what is possible and where limitations exist. A more comprehensive approach to total force deployment is necessary to view the integration of force transportation and the networks required to coordinate force closure.

Within the focus of aerial transport, further research into the large scale use of airlift and the effects of crew and MOG limitations is crucial. This research viewed aircraft fleet capabilities operating free from the constraints of infrastructure and personnel. These variables can become equally if not more constraining, particularly over the course of a lengthy deployment. MOG issues and prohibitive enroute systems can cripple even the most capable airlift fleet. Further research into the available enroute structure and the most vulnerable aspects of its use may contribute greatly to how future airlift fleets are constructed.

www.ingramcontent.com/pod-product-compliance
Lightning Source LLC
Chambersburg PA
CBHW081359280526
45788CB00009B/2922